The French Revolution

An Enthralling Guide to a Major Event in World History

Free limited time bonus

Stop for a moment. We have a free bonus set up for you. The problem is this: we forget 90% of everything that we read after 7 days. Crazy fact, right? Here's the solution: we've created a printable, 1-page pdf summary for this book that you're reading now. All you have to do to get your free pdf summary is to go to the following website:

https://livetolearn.lpages.co/enthrallinghistory/

Once you do, it will be intuitive. Enjoy, and thank you!

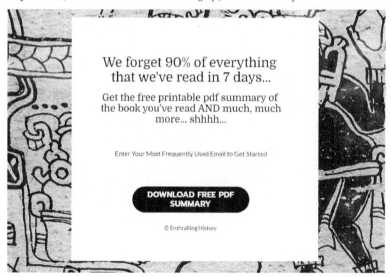

We forget 90% of everything that we've read in 7 days...

Get the free printable pdf summary of the book you've read AND much, much more... shhhh...

Enter Your Most Frequently Used Email to Get Started

DOWNLOAD FREE PDF SUMMARY

© Enthralling History

Table of Contents

Introduction: The French Revolution — What Happened?

The French Revolution stands out as one of the most pivotal moments in history, not just because of what happened in France but also because of how it affected the rest of the world. The undercurrents of what was taking place in France would shake up much of the known world.

As the ideals of the French Revolution spilled outside of French borders, the nations of Europe and the Americas began to absorb them. The lines of European nations were redrawn, while colonial powers, such as Spain and Portugal, lost their hold over their American possessions. Latin America was perhaps the most affected, as country after country in Latin America declared its independence in the aftermath of the French Revolution.

However, even more importantly, the French Revolution disrupted common thought. Before the French Revolution had begun, French intellectuals frequently poked and prodded at the social, religious, and political conventions of the day.

This is perhaps no better demonstrated than in the French Revolution's effect on what was then a centuries-old practice—the Inquisition. The first Inquisition began in the late 12th century, although things really picked up with the Spanish Inquisition, which began in the 15th century. Grand inquisitors were sent from town to town, making inquests into those who were accused of being non-Christians. They had the power and authority to torture and kill if necessary in their quest for "the truth."

It is perhaps a little-known fact, but just prior to the French Revolution, French philosophers like Voltaire played a key role in spreading the word about the abuses and trespasses of the Inquisition. Voltaire would not live to see the French Revolution, but many of his thoughts were put into action during that time and might have helped lead to the end of the Inquisition, which he had so regularly harangued.

Ironically (but perhaps not so coincidentally), the French despot Napoleon Bonaparte brought much of the brutality of the Spanish Inquisition to an end. When his armies conquered Spain, he issued orders to shut it down. The French Revolution's impacts are indeed deep and incredible to contemplate. In this book, we explore the major aspects of the French Revolution and its subsequent impact on the larger world.

Chapter 1: Before the Revolution

"Every time I appoint someone to a vacant position, I make a hundred unhappy and one ungrateful."

-King Louis XIV

To understand the French Revolution, we need to take into account the events that occurred prior to its outbreak. French society had become increasingly unstable in the decades leading up to the revolution. The French Crown had fought a series of losing wars against Britain, the last of which—the Seven Years' War—saw France lose considerable territory in North America, such as Quebec.

This was a humiliation for French pride and proved to be a drain on the French economy as well. The French had to pay the costs accrued from a failed war and suffer the loss of revenue from their former North American colonies. In the meantime, French society was becoming increasingly unequal. There had always been distinct social classes in France, but as the economy was being run into the ground, corruption took hold.

For those who had the extra cash on hand, important posts could be bought. This created a situation in which the wealthy could buy their way into positions of power and lord it over the rest. The worst of this pay-for-play phenomenon occurred in the guilds.

During the Middle Ages and into the early modern period, many European countries had an established set of guilds or trades that certain people did. There were carpenter guilds for carpenters, shipbuilding guilds for shipbuilders, tailor guilds for tailors, and so on and so forth.

These guilds previously only had the best of the best within their ranks. But as corruption set in, it became possible to gain access to a guild by simply buying one's way into it.

One can only imagine the chaos this created when the son of a rich noble could suddenly become a carpenter just because he wanted to be a carpenter, not because he had the skills necessary for that vocation. For the right sum of money, anyone could buy their way into a guild. This caused French trade to become inefficient, stifled free enterprise and creativity, and led to widespread discontent.

Just imagine someone today approaching a hospital board and stating, "Hey, my son really wants to be a doctor." The son doesn't have the right qualifications, but after his rich parents hand over a million dollars, they pull enough strings to get him licensed as a surgeon. Due to this terrible instance of corruption, we now have someone doing open heart surgery who doesn't even know how to use a scalpel!

This was precisely the kind of corruption that had become common practice in the guild systems of pre-revolutionary France. However, even worse was the so-called "sale and purchase of offices." The French had developed a long-standing tradition of government posts and offices being sold to the highest bidder. According to historian Simon Schama, "the sale and purchase of office was more deeply and broadly rooted in France than in any other major power in Europe."

Schama asserts that the practice has its roots in actions undertaken by King Henry IV of France back in 1604 when the French monarchy embarked upon a scheme to sell prestigious government posts to raise much-needed funds for the French treasury. This sort of corruption—the notion that one could buy their way into either positions of power or an esteemed guild—would eventually rot the core of any good society, and that is precisely the sort of thing we see at work in pre-revolutionary France.

As the guilds became worthless, the only way the government could stave off complete economic collapse was by writing off debt through annuities. There were all kinds of government-backed schemes, such as so-called "perpetual annuities," "life annuities," and, at one point, even revertible annuities. It did not matter what gimmick the French king's finance ministers tried, as they were playing with fire. In reality, they were just delaying what would become an inevitable financial collapse.

The French monarchy, due to its extravagance and poor management, had long squandered the resources of what had once been a thriving French presence on the world stage. King Louis XIV, also known as the Sun King, reigned for seventy-two years, from 1643 to 1715. While France emerged as a leading power during his rule, he also set a precedent for how a king should live. Granted, he had the funds to do this, as he made sound reforms early in his reign. However, France became engaged in several major wars, and Louis sought to decrease the nobles' power. As the years passed, Louis XIV needed more money, and he wanted to tax the aristocrats to get it. It was not a popular move, and the taxes ended up being ineffective, with the nobles finding ways to get out of paying them.

King Louis XV had to strengthen the economy in some way, but his taxes on the nobility were not effective either. France fought in more wars. But where Louis XIV won his wars, Louis XV lost many of his. France was in a state of chaos before Louis XVI even took the throne. If France was going to succeed, it needed a strong ruler at the helm.

King Louis XVI was not that strong ruler. This is not to say that Louis XVI was the worst ruler who ever lived. If he had ruled at a different point in history, he likely would have had a semi-successful reign. He could make smart decisions, but he didn't know how to make the people follow his reforms. He also followed in the footsteps of his family, spending money to keep up appearances and engaging in more frivolous activities like hunting.

A great example of this would be his coronation in 1775 when he refused to tone down the extravagance of the ceremony, even after the Controller General of France, Anne Robert Jacques Turgot, advised that he would be wise to do so. Just prior to Louis XVI being crowned, there had been terrible grain riots and unrest in the streets over rising prices. In light of these difficulties, Turgot felt that not only should extravagance be minimized but that it would also serve the king best to hold the coronation in Paris, where the average discontent Parisian could see him, rather than hold the ceremony in the faraway and disconnected opulence of Reims Cathedral.

According to historian Simon Schama, the switch to a more low-key gathering in Paris likely would have saved seven million livres. The cost of having to transport everything, including skilled Parisian artisans, was a major drain on finances.

The costly royal apartments set up temporarily in Reims also sparked tremendous criticism, especially when it was learned that the queen had gone out of her way to install what historian Schama refers to as "English water closets." In other words, this temporary yet costly abode in Reims came decked out with plumbing, including an early version of a functioning toilet. At this time, most French people were stuck using chamber pots.

Such things did not bode well for the new king, who seemed out of tune with the French people from the outset. Besides being costly, some aspects of the ceremony verged on the absurd, such as when sacred oil, supposedly dating back to the first French king (Clovis, King of the Franks), was liberally applied to Louis XVI.

The French king, Louis XVI, would later go on to support the American rebellion against the British Crown, but it was not because he agreed with the American revolutionaries' principles. Far from it. Instead, he simply supported the colonists because it was a way for him to get back at his enemies, the English, who had robbed him of his colonies in the Seven Years' War. For the French ideologues back home, the irony could not have been thicker. The idea that the Americans could achieve the freedom they sought while they were expected to suffer in silence under their own tyrannical king seemed beyond absurd.

As such, the movement to depose King Louis XVI grew. The discord was the most palpable in the French capital of Paris. Exacerbating tensions was a large wave of migrants from the countryside flocking to the capital in search of better work opportunities.

Initially, this seemed to present a potential economic boon, as new factories were developed, and industrialization was encouraged by this large labor pool. The jobs were filled so rapidly by this influx of new arrivals that many of the job seekers had to be turned away, leaving empty-handed. And when work could not be found, the increased population of Paris proved to be more of a burden than a benefit. The French government seemed to shift between trying to aid the newcomers and trying to prohibit them. Many new laws were issued that restricted movement in a last-ditch effort to curtail the steady migration to Paris. However, it was too little, too late, and the French king soon had a large mass of discontented people right on his doorstep demanding that he do something to alleviate their many woes.

And the woes of the poor peasants in France were indeed many. The conditions of the lower classes were shockingly threadbare compared to other European countries of the time. French peasants typically lived in rundown houses that lacked even a proper floor. Rather than wooden floorboards, most of them were just floorless shacks—walls and a roof—roughly assembled on the dirt. The peasants' diet was not much better. They hardly ever had meat, and their meals primarily consisted of bread and perhaps a few vegetables.

It is worth noting that bread played a major part in the French Revolution in many ways. At first glance, the notion that bread was a major factor in a revolution may sound a little absurd, but it is true. The French, especially the French peasants, depended on a steady supply of bread to survive.

And as the prices of bread rose and fell, so did the stability of the French government. There were countless bread riots leading up to the revolution. In January 1789, on the very eve of the French Revolution, bread prices doubled, and the calls for revolutionary reform reached a fever pitch.

When King Louis XVI and his queen, Marie Antoinette, were deposed, the people were heard chanting that they would no longer want for bread because they had just captured the bakers. Crowds were heard rejoicing, "We are bringing back the baker and the baker's wife!"

Such notions were terribly misguided and overly simplistic. If anyone really thought having a captive French king on their hands would give them a lifetime supply of bread, they would soon learn how terribly mistaken they were. The troubles of the French peasants persisted after the king and queen were captured and even after their execution.

Marie Antoinette is often quoted as having said "Let them eat cake" when her ministers pestered her and her husband about the price of bread. However, it is widely believed that she never uttered those words. Still, she was out of touch with what the majority of the French populace was facing, but so were all the other nobles. And in the lead-up to the French Revolution, it seemed that just about everyone had their complaints and criticisms, but very few had any real solutions.

On the eve of the French Revolution, the French government was straining under immense debt. Much of this debt was due to the costs of previous wars. Both the Seven Years' War and the French commitment to supporting the Americans during the American Revolutionary War had racked up considerable debt. France's previously mismanaged policies did not help things either. As it pertained to fiscal responsibility, a big part of the problem lay at the feet of the absolute monarchy. In England, Parliament served as a guardrail when it came to monetary policies. But in France, everything was carried out at the monarch's whim. There were no restrictions in place to hold him back; really, the only thing that could stop him would be a coup or a revolution.

As historian Simon Schama put it, "In France, there was no comparable institution that could act as a dependable watchdog and so reassure future depositors and creditors of government." England had Parliament standing guard, but who would keep the French king in check? It was this fact that made investors more than a little nervous about investing in France.

At any rate, the French government sought to recoup some of its debt by resorting to high taxation. This created more discontent at just about every level of French society. At one point, even the French clergy protested. In 1775, they determined their annual stipends were not sufficient enough to combat inflation and the rise in taxes.

Before the French Revolution, the French government had become corrupt and rotten to its core. It was clear that something had to be done. The sentiments that change was necessary would drive the revolution forward. And French philosophers had been calling for this change for some time.

French philosopher and firebrand Voltaire was at the forefront of this push. Voltaire was a highly influential figure, even though he did not live to see it all play out. Even though it took about another ten years after his death for the revolution to break out, he could sense what was about to happen. Voltaire, thinking that an age of democracy, freedom, and prosperity was about to be ushered in, was envious of those who would live to see it.

In 1764, Voltaire famously declared, "Everywhere the seeds are being sown of an inevitable revolution which I shall not have the joy of witnessing. Happy are the young, for they will see great things!"

Voltaire perished at the age of eighty-three in the year 1778, about ten years prior to the outbreak of the French Revolution. If Voltaire had lived to see the aftermath of the French Revolution, he likely would have regretted his remarks.

As an indication of how much French thought would transfo.
the eve of the revolution, Voltaire, who was very much considere.
liberal during his lifetime, would have been considered a conservative by
the time the French Revolution broke out.

For example, Voltaire railed against the abuses of the Catholic
Church, specifically the inquisitions that were taking place in Spain,
Portugal, and Rome. However, Voltaire was not against religion itself.
On the contrary, he himself professed belief in God and insisted that
religion was good as long as it was natural and not forced on people.
This would be very different from what took place during the French
Revolution.

In the wake of the French Revolution, the church was attacked and
even threatened with annihilation, as Maximilien Robespierre and his
cronies tried to "invent" a new religion they could force upon the whole
French state. This madness was ultimately stopped. Napoleon
Bonaparte, of all people, restored the Catholic Church's hegemony over
France.

Voltaire likely would have looked on in horror as these things played
out. And who knows? Perhaps Voltaire would have been forced to pay a
visit to the guillotine before it was all over. Such a thing would not be
surprising, considering all of the people who were suddenly deemed
expendable due to the irrational whims of fervent revolutionaries.

Voltaire is just one of the heavyweight French thinkers who come to
mind when considering some of the inspirations behind the French
Revolution. However, Voltaire did not advocate for the outright
overthrow of the French monarchy. Instead, he advised a more cautious
approach that would transform the absolutist rule into a constitutional
monarchy.

Voltaire lived in Britain as a young man and absorbed much as it
pertains to the British way of life. He often spoke of his admiration for
the British embrace of merit (no matter how limited it might have been)
while heaping scorn on French nobles who used money and aristocratic
birth to foist their will on others. Early in his career, in the year 1733,
Voltaire made use of his many observations and compiled them into a
piece entitled *Letters on the English*, in which he praised certain aspects
of British society while taking subtle swipes at France.

In one passage, for example, he speaks rather glowingly of British
methods of taxation, stating, "No one is exempted in this Country

n paying certain taxes because he is a nobleman or a

readers back home in France would have readily recognized this statement as an indirect criticism of the French way of life. In France, it was common knowledge that certain members of the nobility and clergy were often exempt from paying taxes. Even though the swipes were subtle, this work and others by Voltaire and his peers enraged the French monarchy. They saw Enlightenment thinkers like Voltaire as nothing but a direct threat to their own authority.

Nevertheless, an undercurrent of intellectual thought bubbled under the surface for some time in France, an undercurrent that would do its utmost to influence and mobilize the unhappy French masses. And the masses were indeed many. France, despite all of its problems, boasted one of the biggest populations in Europe.

Just prior to the revolution, France is said to have had a population of some twenty-eight million people. During this period, Britain barely had a population of ten million. Russia had a population of around thirty million, but one has to keep in mind that Russia's landmass is much larger than that of France. France's current population is about twice as much as it was back then, but modern-day France is also much more capable of coping with a larger population than it was in the late 18th century. Plus, the modern-day French population is more evenly distributed throughout the country.

Pre-revolutionary France found itself low on resources and revenue with a huge, ever-growing population crowding into its cities. The French intelligentsia set to work to address these problems. But little did any of those well-meaning revolutionary ideologues know about the Pandora's box they were about to open.

And in this backdrop, the Estates General would convene. The Estates General was France's legislative body made up to represent the various "estates" of France. The French public of that time was broken up into three main categories. The First Estate was made up of the clergy, the Second Estate the nobility, and the Third Estate comprised the vast bulk of France. The Third Estate was everyone who did not fit into the other two categories; farmers, merchants, shop owners, and blacksmiths, just to name a few, would have all been part of the Third Estate.

The Estates General convened to discuss some of the most pressing problems facing France on May 5th, 1789. The convening of the Estates General was meant to soothe rattled nerves, but all it seemed to do was stir things up. King Louis XVI initiated the discussion, speaking to all of those assembled and attempting to address the many problems the nation faced.

Another important figure, the finance minister, Jacques Necker, spoke before the crowd about the dire circumstances facing the French economy. Necker's go-to solution of enforcing higher taxes predictably fell flat with those who had assembled. Taxes were already high, and it was largely the Third Estate who shouldered the burden.

The Third Estate was upset for another reason. In past sessions of the Estates General, each estate got one vote. The First Estate and the Second Estate tended to side together, leaving the Third Estate, even though it was the most numerous, out in the cold. They wanted to fix things so that every delegate present got a vote. Well, the king had more important things on his mind (taxes), and the discussion of representation was never really talked about.

Frustrated with the situation, members of the Third Estate created a new legislative body, which would become known as the National Assembly. This was all done without the consent of the king. The Third Estate began to refer to themselves as the Communes in reference to their "common" status. They considered their numbers to be of greater significance than any perceived clout or status that the clergy and nobility held.

The gathered representatives of the Third Estate considered themselves the true representatives of the nation, thus forging a true National Assembly to represent French interests. The king sought to shut down what he viewed as an unlawful assembly. He even shut down the meeting hall where the group had convened in the hopes that they would disperse.

However, the Communes simply moved their deliberations to a local tennis court, where they took part in the so-called "Tennis Court Oath," in which they promised not to depart until they had successfully forged a new constitution for their nation. Although no shots had yet been fired, this was indeed the start of what would become an all-out revolution.

Chapter 2: The Storming of The Bastille

"Smuggle out the truth, pass it through all the obstacles that its enemies fabricate; multiply, spread by all means possible her message so that she may triumph; through zeal and civic action counterbalance the influence of money and the machinations lavished on the propagation of deception. That, in my opinion, is the most useful activity and the most sacred duty of pure patriotism."

-Maximilien Robespierre

The French might still recognize Bastille Day as one of their great holidays and hallmarks of their long march toward liberty, but the Storming of the Bastille was by no means a pretty picture. It happened as a result of the restless peasants wanting to arm themselves against the French government.

Before the Bastille, a large fortress and prison, was stormed, the French king had mobilized troops against ongoing bread riots and other demonstrations. He then began cleaning house in his own government. His actions culminated in the termination of Jacques Necker, the finance minister, on July 11th, 1789.

In many ways, Necker had been instrumental in his own demise. He was tasked with fixing the huge debt accrued by France in its effort to aid the American Revolution. Some tried to put the blame on Necker himself, and there was grumbling that he was "cooking the books."

In an effort to come clean on how much was owed, Necker took the step of making the national budget public, which was unusual for an absolute monarchy. Typically, state finances were kept quiet. The memorandum Necker issued was known as the *Compte rendu*. This report shed new light on the French government's state of affairs, alerting the public to all of the dire details of the French economy.

Necker then sought to make taxation more equal by dividing up the taille and capitation taxes. The capitation tax was a poll tax on property, while the taille tax was a more direct form of taxation aimed at the peasant classes in France. While it wasn't unheard of for the more affluent to pay the taille tax, the clergy and nobility typically got out of it by claiming to have a tax-exempt status. This created an increasing hatred of the taille tax, which came to be viewed essentially as a "poor tax" forced upon the lower classes of France.

Although Necker's proposal of reforming the taille tax was popular with many of the poorer French, it alienated the elites, who normally would have been Necker's most important and powerful patrons.

As soon as the people learned that Necker had been terminated, a ripple of panic went through investors. In their minds, the dismissal of the finance minister seemed to indicate the whole country was about to go bankrupt. The elites in France began to raise the alarm.

So, now the poor and the rich were discontented. In the immediate aftermath of Necker's dismissal, which occurred on July 11th, 1789, Paris became ground zero for a revolution.

There was a strange dichotomy in the works, with the National Assembly of France—a special representative body established in the first stages of the French Revolution—seeking to urge calm, even while increasingly upset crowds of people began to gather in the capital. The National Assembly had signed the Tennis Court Oath in direct defiance of the French king, who had ordered them to disband. With this act of defiance, the National Assembly showed that the French monarchy was losing control of this rapidly unfolding situation.

There is nothing worse for a country than to have a mob of unemployed, hungry, and agitated folks roaming throughout the streets, yet that was exactly what Paris, France, looked like at this point in time. And once the people learned of the finance minister's removal, they went into action. Seeming to think that no finance minister meant no control of finances, mobs stormed into toll houses and other tax-collecting institutions, seeking to take back the money they felt had been taken from them.

The king's troops could have fired upon the crowds since they were clearly breaking the law. But as is the case with any breakdown of society, a turning point was reached. Instead of firing on the agitated protesters, the troops shrugged their shoulders, turned their backs, and looked the other way.

With the French soldiers having lost the will to repress their angry countrymen, they opened the door to all kinds of mayhem and lawlessness. Although the French soldiers were unwilling to discharge their weapons to protect the social order, the rabble in the streets was more than willing to seize arms to disrupt it.

On July 13th, 1789, a large crowd assembled in the main town hall in Paris and openly asked for weapons. They insisted they needed these weapons to "protect the city" since the French soldiers had proven themselves unwilling to do so. They were initially met with refusal, but soon enough, administrators began to cave in. It was then agreed that the electors of Paris, who served as representatives, would be allowed to establish a people's militia.

The electors were initially convened to elect the deputies to represent Paris's Third Estate, but in the drama that had unfolded, they became a kind of revolutionary committee that made demands on behalf of the demonstrators. At the behest of the electors, an allotment of rifles and ammunition was distributed to the people, but it was soon deemed not to be worthy of the effort.

The protestors wanted more, and they knew where to get it: the Bastille. The Bastille was a fortress that held prisoners, weapons, and ammunition. The French knew that if they could gain access to the Bastille's armory, they would be well armed. The electors leading the protests ultimately decided to move against the Bastille on the following day, July 14th.

Even though the demonstrators were numerous in number, the storming of the Bastille would not be an easy task. The Bastille stood tall between thick walls and was surrounded by a moat. Initially, the leaders of the mob tried a somewhat diplomatic approach. They stood at the gates of the Bastille and attempted to negotiate with the governor of the Bastille, Bernard-René Jourdan de Launay. They asked him for arms. In the midst of these talks, someone—it is not entirely clear who—opened fire. This led to the whole armed guard at the Bastille opening up on the protesters. Hundreds were killed, but the mob kept coming until the Bastille was overwhelmed.

With so many of their comrades dead, the rage of the protestors was uncontrollable. Right before the protestors were about to break down the doors, Governor de Launay agreed to surrender on the promise that he and those with him would be spared. However, when the Bastille was surrendered, all promises were forgotten.

De Launay was marched outside and horrifically abused. People in the crowd beat him and spit on him. Revolutionary leaders were still trying to figure out what to do with him when Launay, weary of the misery he was being put through, shouted that they should kill him. According to historian Simon Schama, he shouted, "Let me die!"

Launay apparently sought to provoke his death by kicking one of the men closest to him—a fellow whose name comes down to us as Desnot—in the groin. After this outburst, several men leaped on him, tearing him to pieces with swords, daggers, and whatever else they had on hand.

His body was hacked into pieces, and his decapitated head was placed on top of a pike and victoriously thrust into the air by the bloodthirsty crowd. This was an altogether terrible episode, and, in many ways, it was a foreshadowing of the rest of the horror to come.

Along with the desire to acquire weapons, the mob had been partially inspired to storm the Bastille on rumors that it was filled to the brim with prisoners who had dared to speak ill of the regime. In reality, the Bastille is said to have only housed seven prisoners at the time, and none of them were being held for their political views. Word of what happened spread relatively fast, and soon, there were similar demonstrations popping up all over France.

One of the more interesting elements in this early stage of the revolution was the prominent role women played. While it is true that women were generally shut out of the inner circles of revolutionary thought, which forged new civil laws and a constitution, female protesters played a very important role and were quite visible in the streets of France. In the fall of 1789, this was evident when some seven thousand women marched on Versailles, the seat of the French government, where the king resided.

On October 5th, 1789, an angry mob primarily composed of women reacted to high bread prices by marching through the streets of Paris, shouting, "When will we have bread?" This was the title of a protest pamphlet that had been passed out by firebrand intellectuals.

As writer and historian Simon Schama put it in his groundbreaking text *Citizens: A Chronicle of the French Revolution*, "Early on the fifth, the tocsin was rung from the Church of Sainte-Marguerite and, led by a woman beating a drum, a march formed, the crowd shouting the title of the latest pamphlet, *When Will We Have Bread?* As they marched, they recruited women from other districts, many of them carrying cudgels, sticks and knives. By the time they had converged on the Hôtel de Ville the crowd was some six or seven thousand strong."

One can only imagine this strange scene of thousands of women marching with knives, clubs, and, in some instances, sticks, shouting and screaming that they needed bread while liberally abusing their least favorite French monarch, Queen Marie Antoinette.

But why was Marie Antoinette so thoroughly reviled by the French people? This requires some explanation. Initially, the disdain of Marie Antoinette was quite petty. From the start of her public life as queen, many resented the fact that she was not French. As narrow-minded as it sounds, the French public simply did not warm up to the fact that Louis XVI had married a woman who hailed from Austria.

This general disdain was greatly amplified by the French press through a steady series of digs and jabs at her character. All of this negative gossip culminated when the queen was falsely accused of taking an immensely expensive necklace and not paying for it, thereby defrauding the Crown jewelers. This accusation caught on like wildfire in the gossip mills of France, and everyone who already disliked the queen used this piece of gossip to validate their own prejudice.

The accusations were false, and it was later found that the queen's signature had been forged, making it seem as if she had agreed to purchase the necklace when she had not. Nevertheless, Marie Antoinette's reputation had already been ruined, and she would be the butt of jokes and a target of the people's hatred all the way up until she lost her head by way of the guillotine.

Misguided or not, by the time the massive throng of demonstrators arrived at the Hôtel de Ville, their demands had been ratcheted up considerably. Along with complaining about the price of bread, they also demanded that the royal bodyguards, the protectors of the king and queen, be disbanded at once. It might seem an odd demand, but the royal bodyguards had roughed up the crowds on previous occasions.

The crowd also demanded weapons of their own. And they were soon able to get them, as they surged into the city hall and laid siege to a stockpile of weapons. By this point, the women's march had been augmented by a large contingent of men. And this armed group of protesters next marched on the Palace of Versailles.

Marquis de Lafayette attempted to bring order to this chaos. Lafayette is an intriguing character in his own right, and we would be remiss not to speak of him in greater detail. He was born into a wealthy French family and became a commissioned officer when he was still a young teenager. At the outbreak of the American Revolutionary War in 1775, he decided to head to the American colonies and volunteer his services to the Americans.

His efforts were rewarded, and he ended up rising to the rank of general when he was just nineteen years old. After his return to France, he managed to get elected to the Estates General in 1789. Lafayette was a well-known and respected figure, and it was hoped that he would be able to somehow stem the tide of rebellion and bring back some sense of normalcy.

However, he soon became quite alarmed to find that many of his own troops were joining the maddened mob of protesters. Lafayette knew that he could not prevent the march. So, Lafayette made the decision to lead his troops in tandem with the mob as they marched to the Palace of Versailles. As Schama put it, this was done "to ensure that his soldiers were acting for, rather than against, the safety of the royal household."

Since Lafayette could not stop the march outright, he was positioning his reluctant men as shepherds of the protesters, hoping to at least provide enough damage control to prevent an all-out disaster at Versailles. He also made sure the palace was given advance notice of the mob headed its way by sending out a messenger on a fast horse to inform the palace authorities of what was transpiring.

King Louis XVI was actually out hunting when he was informed of the mob's impending arrival. He rushed back to the palace and began to brace himself for the breach. Crowds surged forward, and at one point, they very nearly reached the personal quarters of Marie Antoinette.

A soldier, either on purpose or by accident, had left a gate open. The protesters surged through the opening to gain access to the palace. The mob was heard shouting all kinds of insults toward the queen. Some even shouted that it would be necessary to "cut off her head" and even "fricassee her liver." The palace guard tried to stave them off even though they were entirely overwhelmed.

One guard whose name comes down to us as Monsieur des Huttes was stationed just outside the queen's chamber. He fired a shot into the crowd, hoping he might be able to disperse them. The shot hit one of the protesters. The shot did not cause the protestors to pause. Instead, it sent a fury through the throng, and they surged forward and seized hold of the guard. They supposedly killed this man on the spot.

Another guard by the name of Mimondre de Sainte-Marie tried to talk the crowd down. Once he realized he would be unsuccessful, he began shouting behind the barred doors he guarded. He screamed at the top of his lungs, "The Queen's life is in danger!" He shouted this fateful warning until the mob reached him and silenced him by ending his life.

However, before this man died, his words were heard by those inside, and evasive action was taken. The warning led Marie Antoinette to flee from her quarters, shouting for anyone and everyone who could hear her to help her make her exit. She was led through a secret passageway to the king's room. With nowhere else to go, she banged on the door in desperation.

It took several minutes, but finally, it was opened. The queen was reunited with her husband and her son and daughter, who were hiding inside with their retainers. The head of that brave guard who warned the queen of the threat she faced had his head placed on the tip of a long pike. The head was paraded around the palace grounds as a macabre kind of trophy.

By this time, Lafayette had made his way to the king's quarters and was able to take stock of the situation. Lafayette was flanked by members of the national guard, which had already shown their duplicity. He addressed these men and was able to convince them that he wasn't as bad as the mobs of Paris had let on.

In the French press, the king was blamed for every ill that the average person faced. And he was not only blamed; elaborate conspiracy theories were concocted to make it seem as if the king was intentionally inflicting harm upon the populace. After a crop failure in 1789, a rumor known as the "Famine Pact" went into circulation, declaring that the king and his cohorts were orchestrating an artificially engineered famine to deliberately destroy the peasantry of France.

As absurd as such conspiracy theories might sound, many in France did believe such things to be true. And as soon as one bought into such beliefs, it was no longer just a matter of a monarch who might have made some poor decisions. Instead, many were led to believe that the king was some sort of demonic tyrant hellbent on their own destruction.

Incredibly enough, though, Lafayette's efforts to convince the crowd were somehow successful, and the men who previously had trouble deciding their allegiance suddenly declared their unwavering support for the king of France. Feeling more secure, the king then decided to go to the balcony to address the mob himself. Incredibly, after all of the threats, insults, and deaths of the imperial guard, the crowd was receptive to the king and even showered him with a rousing round of cheers and applause.

You might be shocked to see the sudden change in how people viewed the king. Well, the bar is set pretty low when someone is seen as a monster. If someone has been thoroughly dehumanized and depicted as a horrible monster, it doesn't take much to surprise one's critics. Just a smile and a wave might be all that is necessary to dispel rumors that one is a hellhound with fangs and claws.

Once the king had their attention, he promised his subjects that he would do his best to end the bread crisis and to meet all of their many other concerns and demands. The king had been driven into a corner and was trying to use what was left of his power to instill faith in his people. And during that moment, he succeeded.

But his victory came at a cost. The crowd demanded that the royal family relocate to the French capital. The bullied and harried king felt as if he had no choice but to comply and agreed to leave the safety of his palace at Versailles and head into the thick of things in Paris. The king and his family were marched off to the French capital with the mob of protesters following close behind.

Some of the protestors had heads on pikes, which they gleefully and unabashedly waved in the air, but most simply had their coveted bread impaled on pikes instead. Yes, the giddy crowd, some with bread literally impaled on pikes, exulted in their triumph. Considering they had cornered and cowed the royal family into submitting to their demands, they were heard joyously chanting about how they now had "the baker, the baker's wife, and the baker's lad" in their possession.

However, having King Louis, Marie Antoinette, and their children would not solve all of their problems. Still, this vicious mob felt they had achieved some great feat. They seemed to think they would never go without bread again because they had the perceived producers of their sustenance in their possession. They would soon learn how wrong they were.

Chapter 3: The March toward a Constitutional Monarchy

"The most extravagant idea that can be born in the head of a political thinker is to believe that it suffices for people to enter, weapons in hand, among a foreign people and expect to have its laws and constitution embraced. No one loves armed missionaries; the first lesson of nature and prudence is to repulse them as enemies."

-Maximilien Robespierre

The next major step on the road to revolution was the dismantling of the Ancien Régime (Old Regime). First of all, the notion of France being based on the outdated practice of feudalism was addressed. The National Assembly met in early August to discuss measures for reform. The assembly ultimately decided to get rid of all forms of serfdom, feudal dues, and the tax privileges and exemptions of the elites. However, it must be noted that the National Assembly was not waving a magic wand to get rid of all the debts that were already owed. The intention was that people would continue to pay until these reforms took effect.

This situation back then would be akin to a presidential candidate in the United States today promising to do something just prior to an election to win votes. Many voters might conclude that a vote for this candidate would fulfill such a promise despite the fact that such a promise would take time to go into effect if it ever did.

A similar situation was afoot in France. French citizens were elated at the prospect of debt relief but did not understand the process that it involved. And due to this gross misunderstanding, many refused to pay prior to the reforms even taking effect. This made the financial crisis in France much more severe, as practically all payments ceased. The French government soon went bankrupt as a result.

Nevertheless, once the genie was out of the bottle, there was absolutely no way of putting it back. The peasants were armed, taxes had been absolved, and the old social order had been tossed out right along with it. The French Revolution had begun. But now that revolutionary reform was at hand, what was next? What would be the guiding principles of the revolution? To determine this, the French revolutionaries turned to leading French intellectuals to craft a bill of rights.

Everyone had seen the stunning success of the Americans' Declaration of Independence. The French sought to outdo the Americans with their Declaration of the Rights of Man and of the Citizen, which was made official on August 26th, 1789.

Although the Declaration of the Rights of Man and of the Citizen is often held up as the defining moment of the French Revolution, it was only meant to be a placeholder until a more definite constitution could take shape. The declaration stated that men had natural rights, including the right to life, liberty, and property. The rights declared in the document would influence the French Constitution, which was created a couple of years later, in 1791. There would be another revised constitution made in 1793.

Many are not aware, but a Founding Father of the United States—Thomas Jefferson—was behind the scenes when the Declaration of the Rights of Man and of the Citizen was made. Jefferson was serving in the capacity of a foreign minister on behalf of the US at the time. He was involved in reviewing drafts and was also behind the suggestion of providing a special provision that would enable future constitutional conventions to make amendments if necessary. Ostensibly, the groundwork was being laid for France to be a constitutional monarchy with King Louis XVI as the head.

Yet, paradoxically enough, France's quest for a constitutional monarchy would ultimately end with the French monarch being decapitated. It is a rather blunt way to sum it up yet entirely fitting for what occurred between the years of 1789 and 1792 in France. The first real step, as it pertained to the dismantling of the old order of the Ancien Régime, was the abolishment of feudalism, which occurred on August 4th, 1789.

Then, on August 11th, the revolutionaries decided to do away with the regular tithes requested by the Catholic Church. Instead of having parishioners give tithes to the church, the revolutionaries decided it would be better to have the church receive all funding from the state. But this was not done because the revolutionaries wanted to safeguard the finances of the church; rather, they wanted to have full control of the church.

If the state controlled the purse strings of the church, it would essentially control the church itself. The logic is simple enough. But what the ideologues underestimated was the fervent support the majority of the French people had for the Catholic Church, its institutions, and its traditions. Even if they arbitrarily decided to change the way things were done, it did not mean that everyone else would automatically follow suit.

They might have thought of the priests and nuns who filled up abbeys as nothing more than *faineants* (French for "do-nothings"), but that did not mean that the rest of the population agreed with them. Even so, the ideologues tried to push their luck and take their oppression of the church even further. On November 2nd, 1789, the National Assembly moved in favor of seizing church property and redistributing it as it saw fit.

Although communism was not yet a twinkle in Karl Marx's eye (considering he had not even been born yet), the French were falling back on what would become known as communist-styled principles. However, the worst was yet to come when, on July 12th, 1790, the National Assembly enacted the Civil Constitution of the Clergy, in which they sought to forever meld the functions of the church with civil law.

This move was a far cry from the separation of church and state that had developed in the United States. Instead, the French radicals sought to make the church a distinct arm of the state. They were not particularly religious. They just wished to bend the church to their own ends.

Members of the clergy were pressured to become mouthpieces for the revolution. In November 1790, the National Assembly made it clear to all clergy that if they did not make an official oath of submission to the government, they would be dismissed. Only about a quarter of the priests complied. Those in the more dominantly Catholic parts of France, such as Normandy, Brittany, and the Vendée, were the most steadfast in their resistance. The Catholic Church had much sway over the populations of these regions, and there was considerable pushback there against the French Revolution. The French state's reaction to this resistance was to crack down on the rebels. Priests who were deemed rebellious and contrary were punished, exiled, or even put to death.

It was in this backdrop of this turmoil that the political club of radicals known as the Jacobins came to prominence. The Jacobins were just one of many political clubs that had arrived on the scene. They had originated from a caucus within the Third Estate.

As mentioned before, France was broken up into three basic divisions of society. The First Estate was made up of the nobility. The Second Estate consisted of the clergy. And the Third Estate was made up of the vast bulk of the country, from the poorest of the poor to the more prosperous, non-noble shopkeepers and skilled artisans.

A French revolutionary ideologue named Abbé Sieyès made the most use of this state of affairs. He knew the Third Estate shouldered much of the national burden and that the people were upset. His political pamphlet titled "What is necessary that a nation should prosper?" pointed out the Third Estate was not just a separate class of French society but also the vast majority of the people and essentially the "nation itself."

He argued that since the true blood of the nation was in the Third Estate, who worked and toiled the hardest, the other two estates were nothing more than parasites sucking the Third Estate dry. This caricature of French society was portrayed by various illustrations of a poor and decrepit member of the Third Estate with a member of the clergy and a member of the nobility on their back.

This simplistic message of the Third Estate being forced to carry the load—the full burden of France's problems—truly resonated with the masses and became a lasting theme throughout the French Revolution.

Sieyès also argued that since the Third Estate represented the nation, then those outside of the Third Estate were not worthy of French citizenship. They were nothing more than corrupt, parasitical wasters of life and limb.

As Sieyès put it, "It is impossible to say what place the nobility and clergy ought to occupy in the social order. This is equivalent to asking what place should be assigned to a malignant disease which preys upon and tortures the body of a sick man."

The political clubs—especially the Jacobins—got quite a bit of mileage out of these stinging critiques of French society. The Jacobins thrived on this kind of rhetoric and sought to exploit it to the best of their advantage. They frequently met in a Dominican convent of the same name; thus, they became colloquially known as the Jacobins or the Jacobin Club.

By August of 1790, when the first reforms of the French Revolution were taking hold, the Jacobins of Paris numbered around 1,200. The Jacobins would meet on a regular basis in a building that used to be a church—that aforementioned Dominican convent—the Rue Saint-Honoré. It is ironic that the Jacobins met in a church for their meetings would later take on the form of a church function.

But instead of declaring the glories of God, those who stood before the podium expounded upon the rights of man. As the French were minimizing the role of their traditional Christian religion, they were seeking new solace in the quasi-religious philosophies of political clubs like the Jacobins. As we will see, the French intellectuals would use these philosophical movements as a replacement for religion and other traditions of the Old Regime.

Historian Simon Schama perhaps put it best when he described the Jacobin clubs as a mixture "between a church and a school." This is an apt description. The ideologues were doing their best to expound upon and teach their philosophies to those in attendance, and the insistence that all Jacobins adhere to those philosophical ideals became so intense and extreme that one could say that the members of the Jacobin Club became religious.

It has long been pointed out that human beings seem to have developed religion and philosophy for a reason. The second that one is thrown out, it is not long before it is replaced by another. The same thing occurred in communist Russia when the Christian Church was supplanted by a religious adherence to the communist ideal. For the most part, it seems that humans need something larger than themselves to focus on, whether it is a belief in an eternal, infinite God, the cult of communism, or the zealous implementation and adherence to revolutionary ideals. There is just an innate desire in us to follow something.

These political clubs were the first rudimentary efforts to provide the French mind and soul something they could latch onto in their search for meaning and self-discovery. The Jacobins were looking for something, but there were also those who were working under the nose of the French king who thought they could redirect the Jacobins toward embracing the French monarchy again. And Honoré-Gabriel Riqueti, Comte de (Count of) Mirabeau (more commonly just known as Mirabeau), was one of them.

Mirabeau was a deputy for the Third Estate. He represented the cities of Aix and Marseilles. During the first stage of the French Revolution, he rose to become a key figure in the French government.

Mirabeau is a complicated figure. Although he supported the establishment of a constitutional monarchy, he also insisted that the reforms that allowed for free speech, free press, and the like remain in place. Mirabeau supported the reforms, but he also wisely knew that once these rights were established, there would be no way to roll them back. At the same time, he advocated for the monarchy—even if it were a constitutional monarchy—to remain in place.

Mirabeau was a voice of pragmatic reason known for the rather gifted manner in which he could calm the nerves of agitated and angry crowds. On one occasion, he was able to talk sense into a crowd of agitated rioters in Marseilles. They were angry over the high prices of bread, but Mirabeau reminded them of how pointless their own actions were in the situation.

Addressing the angry mob directly, he reasoned, "Let us first consider bread. At the present time, dear friends, since wheat is expensive everywhere, how could it be cheap at Marseille?" It was a simple enough statement, but it brought some rationality back to the rioters. The whole country was facing high prices, so why did they feel the need to throw a fit over it? Mirabeau's simple logic seemed to sink in, and the rioters of Marseilles soon dispersed.

Mirabeau was a skilled navigator who often strode two worlds, with one foot in the royal palace working with the king and the other in the streets with the common people whom he claimed to champion.

As the tug of war between the king and the revolutionaries became more and more intense, Mirabeau suggested making some of the leading Jacobins members of the king's inner circle. In an apparent effort to reverse the old adage of "If you can't beat them, join them," Mirabeau was basically suggesting, "If you can't beat them, recruit them."

But he was not merely wanting to make nice with the Jacobins. He was wise enough to realize that once the Jacobin leadership was forced to deal with the problems of the French government firsthand—in other words, attempt to find solutions to the problems rather than just endlessly complain about them—they would understand that the issues facing the French were bigger than the monarchy and the political clubs. Mirabeau believed the Jacobins would have just as hard of a time solving them as the French government was having.

As Mirabeau sagely wrote, "The people have been promised more than can be promised; they have been given hopes that it will be impossible to realize. The expense of the new regime will actually be heavier than the old, and in the last analysis the people will judge the revolution by this fact alone—does it take more or less money? Are they better off? Do they have more work? And is that work better paid?"

In hearing Mirabeau's prediction of how the revolutionaries would be even worse administrators than the king's advisers, we can almost hear echoes of former US President Ronald Reagan's simple assessment, "Are you better off than you were four years ago?" Of course, Reagan was referring to a previous presidential administration, while the French were posed with the much more formidable task of assessing the wreckage and aftermath of their scrapping much of the former protocols of the Ancien Régime.

After the French shook off the previous constraints of absolute monarchy, they would have to ask that same question: were they better off? For many, the answer would be a clear and decisive no. Instead of having a better life, the French Revolution and its terrible aftermath would make the lives of many far worse than anyone could have imagined.

It is true that the noble ideals of the French Revolution would begin the framework of a more just and equal society, but it would take quite some time before they were actually put into practice. Ironically, the enlightened despotism of Napoleon Bonaparte would see some widescale implementations of the revolutionary reforms. Of course, he also looked out for his own best interest. For instance, he enforced slavery in French colonies after it had been abolished in 1794.

The Rights of Man and of the Citizen proclaimed the need for equality, freedom of speech, and representative government. And for a time, things looked promising. But ultimately, just about none of the declaration's promises were fulfilled. The whole notion of freedom of speech would become a joke since the French could not go against the ideals of the French Revolution; if they did, they might face arrest or even lose their head.

Mirabeau was perhaps more clear-headed than most since he was able to understand these ramifications before they played out. While others were gripped in revolutionary fervor and could not see much further than the tip of their nose, Mirabeau sagely understood what the end result of all of this tumult might be.

The monarch, King Louis XVI, would have very little to do with these reforms. In fact, King Louis attempted to escape the country in June 1791. These efforts were actually presaged by an earlier event that took place on April 18th, in which the couple was thwarted when they attempted to make a trip to St. Cloud. According to historian Simon Schama, it was on the Monday of Holy Week that the queen and king attempted to make a break for it.

They were blocked by an angry crowd, and once again, their own guard turned on them. An indignant Louis, who had just given in to many demands, declared his amazement that he, who had just granted such freedoms to the French people, was being denied his. The king was indeed a virtual prisoner, and even as he protested, his own guards hurled abuse at him. One even went as far as to call him a "fat pig" whose appetite was draining France's limited resources.

Ultimately, the king and his entourage had no choice but to give up their attempt to leave Paris and head back to their quarters. Yes, the baker, the baker's wife, and the baker's lad (not to mention the baker's daughter as well) were being held hostage by the French revolutionaries who refused to give them up. Nevertheless, knowing that escape just might be their only hope to get out of this ordeal alive, the royal family and their inner circle spent the next couple of months meticulously planning their next attempt.

This time, they would depart in the middle of the night under cover of darkness. In the king's and queen's eyes, it seemed that fleeing would be the only way they could restore their freedom and the monarchy. And just after midnight, on June 20th, 1791, the royal family, in full disguise, fled the Hôtel de Ville right under the nose of the unhelpful palace guards. They had their own royal detachments of troops shepherding them along the way, but even these men could not be entirely depended on. The royals didn't have much of a choice, though, and in this charged atmosphere of intrigue and animosity, just about everyone's sympathies were suspect.

Even worse, as they rode along in their carriage, local villagers began to recognize the king. Even though the king was in disguise, he was quite hard to miss since his face was printed on French currency. Ultimately, a local postmaster named Jean-Baptiste Drouet decided to call the king out, stopping the royal entourage in Sainte-Menehould and loudly proclaiming that the mystery guests were none other than the fleeing royals.

He actually rode ahead of the group and alerted local authorities. They were held in the town of Varennes at the mayor's residence, where they were made to await their arrest and transfer back to the capital.

After the king and queen were captured and returned to Paris, the façade of an all-powerful absolute monarch was finally dropped. It was hard for the people to trust the king as an authority figure after his embarrassing attempt to flee Paris in secret became known. As historian Simon Schama put it, this latest debacle only seemed to accomplish "the annihilation of the royal mystique." Whatever respect the king might have had left was lost after this failed attempt to flee. Eventually, King Louis and his wife, Marie Antoinette, were arrested and put on trial as traitors of the state.

Prior to their ultimate downfall, attempts were made to prop them up. On July 15th, 1791, the National Assembly decided to absolve the king of wrongdoing and go forward with plans to have King Louis made the head of a constitutional monarchy. However, this move created much anger, and soon a multitude of Parisians were out in force protesting.

On July 17th, protesters gathered at the grounds of Champ de Mars on the west side of Paris. Speeches were given, and petitions were signed, all denouncing the ruling that had been made. The demonstrations quickly got out of hand, and the National Guard was called out, with none other than the Marquis de Lafayette leading them. Lafayette was also accompanied by the mayor of Paris, Jean Sylvain Bailly.

Upon their arrival, the crowd almost immediately turned on the guardsmen. The increasingly agitated protesters shouted and hurled stones at the troops. At one point, one of the guardsmen fired his weapon. This action then set the ball in motion, and soon several of the troops were firing into the crowd.

Absolute pandemonium ensued as the demonstrators scattered. Once the smoke cleared, many lay dead. It has been estimated that as many as fifty of the protesters were killed, with many more wounded. Nevertheless, despite the ensuing backlash against this atrocity, the push toward the establishment of a constitutional monarchy went ahead as planned. And the First French Constitution would be put forward on September 3rd, 1791.

This is significant because it was the first effort made by the revolutionary government, under the auspices of the Legislative Assembly, to finalize the new proposed framework of French society in writing. This constitution was heavily influenced by the European Enlightenment and the American Revolution. However, many of the notions conceived within it already seemed somehow out of step with the rapid pace of events that were occurring on the ground.

The king was backed into a corner and forced to concede to virtually all demands. He even had his official title changed. According to this document, he was transformed from "King of France" to simply "King of the French." To the casual observer, this might not seem like that much of a difference. But it made all of the difference in the world.

When Louis was the "King of France," he was the absolute monarch whose rule was unquestioned. But as "King of the French," he had been rendered king only by the good graces of the French people, who allowed him to be king, not to lord it over them as a divine right but in order to safeguard the interests and will of the people.

So far, the turmoil of France had been contained within its borders, but it would soon spill out to affect the rest of the world. On January 17th, 1792, Austrian Emperor—and brother of Marie Antoinette—Leopold II issued demands for the French to leave territory they had seized in Alsace and to release the royal family from their house arrest. On February 7th, a formal alliance was made between Austria and Prussia.

The French issued counterdemands, asking the Austrians not to interfere with French affairs and respect the previous Treaty of Versailles of 1756. The Treaty of Versailles had made the French and Austrians allies, but this treaty had been forged during different times. Nevertheless, the French revolutionaries issued an ultimatum that Leopold II honor this treaty, giving him until March 1st to confirm his commitment to do so.

In one of the strange ironies of history, Leopold II abruptly passed away on March 1ˢᵗ, right before the deadline was set to expire. Leopold was succeeded by his son Francis. Francis would not honor the deadline imposed by the French any more than his father. His silence was interpreted to suggest his own intention for war.

In April 1792, the armed forces of France were sent to take on the forces of Prussia and Austria on the premise that some sort of counter-revolutionary alliance was being created to end the revolution. War was officially declared on Austria on April 20ᵗʰ, which led to Austria's ally Prussia declaring war on France that June. This group was known as the First Coalition.

Things would come to a head in July of 1792 when the Duke of Brunswick threw in his lot with the Austrians and led a Prussian force to invade French territory. This would lead to the seizure of the French city of Verdun on September 2ⁿᵈ. The next year would bring even more shocking developments for France. On January 21ˢᵗ, 1793, King Louis XVI was executed by guillotine.

Chapter 4: The Execution of Louis XVI and the First Republic

"Beware of letting yourselves be carried away by false pity. Your enemies will not spare you, if they have their way. No one abhors bloodshed more than I do, but if you do not want a veritable sea of blood, you must exact a few drops yourselves. To reconcile the public welfare with the needs of humanity, I propose that you decimate the counter-revolutionary members of the Commune, the magistrature, the departments and the National Assembly."

-Jean-Paul Marat

After war broke out with Austria and Prussia, the revolutionaries viewed the royal family as a liability at best and potential traitors at worst. This largely stemmed from the fact that the queen was related to the Austrian Crown, and it was believed that if the royals were not in direct cahoots with France's enemies, they were providing their enemies with an incentive to attack them.

This was seemingly all but proved when the commander of the Austro-Prussian forces, the Duke of Brunswick, fired off a manifesto on July 25th, 1792, in which he unequivocally stated that the forces at his command intended to intervene in France's affairs and forcefully restore the king's lawful authority. It also went as far as to warn that if the king and queen were in any way harmed, there would be widespread retribution.

Although this threat was issued in an effort to safeguard the royals, it had the opposite effect. Instead of taking care not to harm their hostages, the more radical revolutionaries took it as a reason to get rid of them. The Brunswick Manifesto only served to confirm the suspicions of the revolutionaries that the king and queen were liabilities that needed to be dispatched with posthaste.

On August 9th, the Legislative Assembly began to speak of dispatching the imprisoned monarch. But even though the king was in a poor position to fight back, getting rid of him would be no easy task. There were still many who feared and perhaps took the Duke of Brunswick's warning to heart that the repercussions of taking direct action against the king would be too great.

Nevertheless, the louder rabble-rousers were able to convince the assembly to act. After several hours of debate, it was determined that Louis would be put on trial. But the words of the delegates had to be matched with force. So, on August 10th, they sent out the Jacobin National Guard, which was augmented by mobs of rioters, to the Tuileries Palace, where the king was being guarded by 950 of his loyal Swiss Guards.

It is said that once the mob was at the gates of Tuileries, Queen Marie Antoinette was the most determined to make a last stand. She is said to have declared, "Better let ourselves be nailed to the walls of the Palace than to leave it." But her husband did not agree. Instead, he decided that in order to avoid more bloodshed, he should allow himself to be escorted to the assembly to answer the charges being leveled against him. As the king was led to the assembly, the mob turned on the Swiss Guards.

The Swiss Guard had loyally stood their ground, but upon receiving an order from the king, they returned to their barracks. As they attempted to stand down, the infuriated crowd moved in and began to literally shoot them in the back.

The king, the queen, and their children were imprisoned in a fortress called the Temple. This fortress was old even then and purportedly was used by none other than the Knights Templar (thus the name "Temple").

Perhaps it was a bad omen for those hauled inside its walls since the Templars had met a terrible fate when the French king decided to dispatch with them and disband their order in the 14th century. Behind the thick walls of the Temple, the king and queen were completely isolated and cut off from the outside world. All correspondence was forbidden, thereby ensuring that there would be no word as to their condition to friendly outside powers.

The surviving Swiss Guard were either imprisoned or killed in the streets. In September, gruesome events began. After rumors circulated that the prisoners were plotting to link up with an invading army, massacres broke out. Some prisoners were killed on the spot, while others were treated to a tribunal at the gates of the prison. If they were found guilty, which most were, they were walked out to be killed by the bloodthirsty mob that had gathered outside.

On September 21ˢᵗ, 1792, the assembly gathered to officially abolish the monarchy and declare the government a republic. Thus ended the farce of France's constitutional monarchy. Even the manner in which Louis was to be addressed had changed. He was no longer king; instead, he was called Louis Capet.

This name harkened back to Louis's ancestor, Hugh Capet, who became king in the year 987, starting what would be known as the Capetian line. King Louis XVI took offense to this perceived abrogation of his title, as it made him a citizen, not a king. When the mayor of Paris, Aubin Bigore du Chambon, addressed him as such, Louis indignantly replied, "I am not Louis Capet. My ancestors had that name, but I have never been called that."

In the meantime, the French war front received a significant and unexpected boon on September 20ᵗʰ when the French forces scored a decisive victory at the Battle of Valmy. The French, in many ways, viewed their stand at Valmy as their last stand. The Austrians had already descended like an avalanche, taking the towns of Longwy and Verdun. It seemed as if they were on a steady march to Paris itself.

As such, the French defenders viewed Valmy as their "Thermopylae." The battle was deemed a must-win in order to stop the approaching Austrians from reaching the French capital. Despite heavy French losses, the French lines held, and the Austrians were repulsed. This victory would indeed become a major turning point in the French Revolutionary Wars.

Incidentally, the famed German poet and playwright Johann Wolfgang von Goethe was traveling with the Austro-Prussian army and took note of just how demoralized the body of troops had become. It seemed that everyone at all levels knew what a colossal disaster Valmy was going to be. Goethe later recalled that since he was known as a wordsmith, it was requested of him to put words to what happened. Goethe could not help but proclaim, "From this place and this time forth commences a new era in world history, and you can all say that you were present at its birth."

One can only imagine what it would have been like if the French defenders had failed. Perhaps the Austrians would have marched on Paris. Perhaps the royal family would have been rescued by Marie Antoinette's former countrymen. But that was not how history played out.

Instead of Brunswick being able to make good on his threats of aggression, he was forced to order the troops under his command to pull back. The fate of the First Coalition would receive another blow on November 6th when they lost the Battle of Jemappes. The French got hold of a good chunk of what had been the Austrian-controlled Netherlands.

On that same fateful day of September 20th, 1792, the Legislative Assembly previously governing France was dissolved, and the National Convention was established in its place. The National Convention sought the complete removal of the French monarchy, which was officially done on September 21st. The new French Republic was declared on September 22nd.

The French royal family remained in prison with no hope of rescue on the horizon (the supposed rescuers were actually fleeing in the other direction). On January 17th, 1793, the former French king, Louis XVI, was found guilty of treason after a lengthy trial and handed a death sentence. Since all court proceedings were decided and rehearsed beforehand, this "trial" was for demonstrative purposes only. There was never any hope of the king being acquitted.

Nevertheless, the king's sentence was carried out on January 21st, 1793. Louis was awakened in the darkness of the early morning. After being allowed to have his last confession with his priest, he was then put in a carriage and driven off to the chopping block.

He asked beforehand that he be spared the indignity of having his hair cut off—a typical prerequisite of one who was about to have a giant blade cleave through their neck. But even this simple request was denied. After his hair was cut and final adjustments to the guillotine were made, the deposed king gave one last address to the crowd.

Staring out at the vast multitude that was eagerly awaiting his death, King Louis XVI declared, "I die innocent of all the crimes laid to my charge; I pardon those who have occasioned my death; and I pray to God that the blood you are going to shed may never be visited on France." The rest of the monarch's words were subsequently drowned out when drummers were ordered to furiously beat out a military march.

Those who were in charge of the toppled monarch's execution obviously did not want to give the king any chance to try and change the hearts and minds of the French populace. Resigned to his fate, King Louis XVI was directed to submit to the guillotine. With one quick pull of a cord and the even quicker hiss of a rapidly descending blade, the king's head was chopped clean off.

When King Louis XVI lost his head, the heads of state in the rest of Europe were appalled and horrified. They didn't want the revolutionary ideals to spread to their countries, especially if it meant losing their lives in the process. They were ready to go to war. France's National Convention anticipated as much and decided to preempt those foreign powers by making declarations of war on the Netherlands and Britain. Britain and the Netherlands reciprocated and were soon joined by others, principally Spain, Portugal, Tuscany, and Naples, which would all take part in the War of the First Coalition.

There were those in the French government who felt that external threats could be used to strengthen internal factions. The political faction known as the Girondins sought to unify French nationalistic feelings and sentiments during these calls for war. But instead of uniting the French in patriotic fervor, there were protests and even riots in Paris when attempts were made to establish a draft.

The radical group of French revolutionaries known as the Jacobins were largely in charge of the National Convention. The Jacobins had even less love for traditional institutions than their peers. In their efforts of radical transformation, they even went as far as to rename the months of the year and the days of the week. The week was also extended to ten days rather than seven. This was done in the hopes that it would obscure the traditional Christian Sunday by placing it in the middle of a full week of work and recreation.

Yes, atheistic and agnostic French elitists had seized control, and thinking they knew better than the French masses they claimed to champion, they sought to "cure" them of their religious superstition by completely subsuming and burying their impulses for it. Besides these absurd reforms, they also kicked off what would become known as the Reign of Terror, a time when they brutally persecuted anyone they perceived not to be on board with their agenda.

Ever since the storming of the Bastille, the French, regardless of their social class, were concerned with security and safety. The riotous mobs of the revolution never really died down, and spontaneous eruptions of animalistic rage seemed possible at any moment. This was the case in March 1793 when a mob of peasants rose up in the Vendée and launched a vicious assault on the local administration.

One eyewitness to these events, a seven-year-old boy named Germain Bethuis, later gave a disturbing account of what transpired that morning. Bethuis stated, "By now the sun had burnt off the mist to reveal a compact swarm of thousands of peasants, armed with pitchforks, skinning knives, billhooks, sickles, and more than a few hunting guns." As Germain remembered it, "Their wild cries alone were enough to spread terror."

Yes, it would be shocking for anyone to deal with a maddened mob of hundreds of angry, irrational, and hungry people. Even though attempts were made to reason with the crowd and meet some of their demands, they soon ran riot and began looting any targets associated with the local administrators. Even the clergy were not spared in this onslaught. A local priest by the name of Pierre Letort was cornered and viciously stabbed in the face multiple times.

But soon, France faced even more pressing issues than internal threats. France's foreign adversaries were poised to take advantage of France's internal turmoil. The most pressing problem was the threat of Austria. French troops were being demolished on battlefields in Louvain and in the Rhineland. The lack of central authority meant that any concerted action was often lost in a hopeless mire of bureaucratic bickering and inefficiency among the various factions leading the revolution.

Something had to be done to bring stability to this chaos. Henri-Maximin Isnard, who led the political club known as the Girondins, suggested the establishment of a committee that could see to the public's safety from both internal and external threats, the latter of which Isnard and his colleagues had expounded upon at great length in late 1791. In one exchange, Isnard went as far as to put France in the crosshairs of foreign aggression.

As Isnard put it, "The French have become the foremost people of the universe. So their conduct must now correspond to their new destiny. As slaves they were bold and great; are they to be timid and feeble now that they are free?"

Henri-Maximin Isnard and his colleagues were beginning to see their revolution not just as a localized French concern but also as one of great importance on the world stage. It was no longer enough to topple their absolute ruler. They also had to consider taking action against the other monarchs of Europe, such as those in Britain, Austria, and Russia.

The French Revolution was transforming into a crusade against absolutism itself, and the French revolutionaries began to see themselves at the center of this struggle for freedom. They began to feel they were engaged in a zero-sum game. Either they put the monarchs of Europe in their proper place, or they would be inevitably crushed by the foreign heads of state who were aligning against them.

Jacques Pierre Brissot, who was in attendance during these grave discussions, seconded this fear. As historian Schama put it, "Brissot sketched out the features of a vast conspiracy extending throughout Europe, designed to isolate and cripple French power forever. Posing a series of rhetorical questions, he put the pieces of the puzzle in place. Why had Russia suddenly made peace on its eastern frontier with Turkey if not to concentrate on something sinister? Why had the King of Sweden, a known correspondent of the Queen's since his visit to France in the 1780s, mobilized his armies? Why indeed had those arch-enemies Austria and Prussia fallen into each other's arms at Pillnitz? The answer to all these questions was a dagger pointing directly at the heart of the only truly free nation of men in the Old World."

The leading lights of the French Revolution could see the writing on the wall. They were weak at home and faced dire threats abroad since a vast coalition was forming against them. They needed to forge a special political body to tackle all of these threats. It was for this reason that the Committee of Public Safety was forged. This committee was officially established on April 6th, 1793.

The Committee of Public Safety, which was made up of twelve deputies, was given the power to direct the armed forces of France and govern the French nation. But its domestic investigations into the French citizenry and rooting out supposed internal enemies of the state would make this twelve-man committee infamous. The committee was tasked with keeping France "safe," and in the eyes of the revolutionaries, anyone who spoke out against the revolution was considered a danger to the state. The Committee of Public Safety considered itself to be the guardrail of the French Revolution. It was ready and willing to strike anyone who dared step out of line.

Jacobin firebrand Jean-Paul Marat had long been an unofficial mouthpiece of the Jacobin Club through his popular paper *L'Ami du Peuple* or, as it translates into English, *The Friend of the People*. His paper became famous during the height of the French Revolution, as it launched brutal attacks on the king and queen of France, becoming the most popular vehicle of popular discontent. Marat himself was dubbed the "Friend of the People."

However, the Girondins did not appreciate Marat and felt that his hostile and often violent rhetoric was helpful, especially since he targeted fellow members of the revolutionary elite. The tensions in France were so high that the revolutionaries were more than ready to turn their wrath on each other. The political convention subsequently erupted into chaos, with Girondins like Marguerite-Élie Gaudet, Maximin Isnard, and François Buzot heaping their abuse upon the Jacobin leader.

In order to understand the Girondins' point of view, it is important to understand their origins and what they stood for. The Girondins first came about in 1791 during sessions of the Legislative Assembly. The group was forged by a prominent French lawyer named Jacques Pierre Brissot. Because of him, the Girondin faction was initially dubbed the "Brissotins." It was only later when it was noted that most of the membership of this faction hailed from Bordeaux, situated in what was known as the Gironde department, that the group came to be popularly recognized as the Girondins.

The Girondins advocated early on for an end to the absolute monarchy in favor of a republican government. Even so, they were considered moderates or at least far less radical than some of their Jacobin colleagues. The Girondins spoke at length of their desire for what they viewed to be a free France in which liberty and personal merit were of the utmost importance. And they viewed a republican government, with elected representatives, as the best system to ensure that these freedoms were protected.

At the same time, the Girondins cast a wary eye on their more radical colleagues in Paris who were calling not just for reform but also the leveling of French society. The Girondins sought a peaceful exit for the king—perhaps even clemency—whereas the more radical factions insisted the king must be killed. Since the king was eventually executed, the more moderate Girondin approach had clearly gone unheeded. Nevertheless, the Girondins continued to voice their concerns against the more radical mouthpieces at work in Paris, such as Jean-Paul Marat, whom his supporters had dubbed the "Friend of the People."

Just as a demonstration of how petty the barbs were, at one point, one of the fellow delegates at the convention quipped that the podium should "be disinfected after every speech by the Friend of the People." So, as much as we might want to assert that the politics of today are dire and extreme, all one has to do is look at the politics of the French Revolution, which took place well over two hundred years ago, and realize that politics has always been complicated. In fact, it was worse back then, as we will see with Marat's story.

Politics is often compared to a blood sport, and when adequate guardrails are not in place, things get out of control quickly. And in France in the 1790s, those guardrails were shattered. Gaudet was chirping that Marat was a "croaking toad," while Marat shouted that Gaudet was a "vile bird." As childish and juvenile as some of the exchanges sound, they were also dangerous since those slinging these barbs were angling to have their opponents not just mocked but also disgraced and possibly even killed.

Most importantly, the Girondins wished to get an indictment for Marat. They claimed he was inciting violence, and to prove their point, all they had to do was pull up his writings. Simon Schama described their tactics well when he stated, "The Girondins collected evidence from Marat's writings to show that he had violated the integrity of the Convention by calling for violent attacks on its membership."

These assertions led to a nineteen-page indictment, which was handed over to the Revolutionary Tribunal. This was a special court that had been created by the National Convention in March of 1793. It was specifically designed to try those who were dubbed to be enemies of the revolution. In other words, it tried those who were accused of engaging in counter-revolutionary activities.

The Girondins had essentially charged that Marat was stirring up violence and insurrection against the revolutionary government. As historian Simon Schama put it, "The Girondins collected evidence from Marat's writings to show that he had violated the integrity of the Convention by calling for violent attacks on its membership."

The inflammatory articles crafted by Marat in his newspaper were known for their over-the-top style and explosive language. Jean-Paul Marat, for his part, claimed that his words were being taken out of context and that not everything he said should be taken literally.

Of course, such things are open to interpretation. For example, Marat wrote of his "regret" over the fact that "a few hundred heads had been spared so as to preserve hundreds of thousands of innocents." Yes, his words can be literally interpreted as an advocation for violence here, but they can also be seen as rhetoric used to make a point.

At any rate, the indictment went forward, and Marat went to trial. But if the Girondins thought they had their arch-nemesis on the ropes, they were gravely mistaken. Rather than tarnish his image, the perceived political persecution of the stalwart Jacobin raised his profile and made him more popular than ever before.

When he appeared in court, he received a standing ovation. One can only imagine the shock and dismay of the Girondins to see the man they had targeted being showered with a spontaneous eruption of praise. And by the time Marat was given a chance to speak his peace, it was all but over. Marat's greatest gift was his words, and his defense was so brilliant and precise that even the Girondin-selected judges were swayed to take his side.

To the Girondins' chagrin, Marat was acquitted. Rather than going to prison or facing the guillotine, Marat left the courtroom a hero, and a veritable parade followed him through the streets. In celebration of Marat's acquittal, the Jacobins held a grand celebration on April 26th, in which it seemed that all of France was in attendance.

The Girondins had become increasingly unpopular. Their unpopularity was not helped when, in early May, they argued against price controls for grain. At this point, the political fortunes of the Girondins began to dim considerably. On May 16th, Isnard was made the head of the National Convention, and it was through his efforts that a last-ditch effort was made to turn the party's political fortunes around.

Maximin Isnard was radical in his approach, suggesting that a plot was underway to disband the National Convention outright. At one point, Isnard addressed the members of the National Convention and painted a rather dire picture of the future of France if such plots were not foiled. Isnard shouted out to those assembled, "I tell you, in the name of the whole of France, that if these endless insurrections should cause harm to the parliament of the nation, Paris will be annihilated, and men will search the banks of the Seine for signs of the city."

The Jacobins began to claim that the Girondins were responsible for a counter-revolutionary conspiracy. The Girondins were ultimately expelled from the National Convention and placed under house arrest, losing any influence they had left that June.

There was growing anger among those who felt politically excluded, and on June 13th, one of those took matters into her own hands. Her name was Charlotte Corday. She hailed from a family in the French region of Normandy. After the Girondins were disbanded, many Girondin exiles appeared in Normandy and spread the news of their alleged political persecution. Their accounts stirred up the hearts of many, and Corday was inspired to act. She sympathized with the Girondins, who tried to stop the violence from spreading. She traveled to Paris and tracked down Marat.

She arrived at his door on the morning of July 13th and demanded an audience with him. She lied, claiming that she had information about traitors in Normandy. Although she was turned away, Marat admitted her when she returned that evening. Marat gave her an audience while he soaked in the bath (he had a bad skin disorder). Corday gave him the names of Girondins but then plunged a knife into his chest. Hearing his screams, Marat's fiancé, Simonne Evrard, ran into the room. She placed her hand on the wound in an attempt to prevent his life's blood from pouring out.

However, it was no use. Charlotte Corday, in her unbridled rage, had struck home, plunging the knife into an artery, and Marat bled to death. This high-profile assassination ultimately played into the hands of the Jacobins, giving them more reason to institute harsh measures for the "safety" of the populace. The Friend of the People had been struck down, and now the Committee of Public Safety had to make sure that order was restored.

On July 27th, 1793, the firebrand Jacobin revolutionary Maximilien Robespierre was made a member of the committee. This group, which had been established for safety, would become the enforcers of the Reign of Terror since it was up to them to execute any decrees that were made by the National Convention.

Interestingly, Robespierre, a card-carrying Jacobin, was initially suspicious of the committee since it had been established by Isnard, who was a Girondin. Robespierre initially wondered if the committee was a bureaucratic power grab on the part of the Girondins. However, Robespierre would be seduced by the committee's ability to reestablish centralized control over official, state-sanctioned coercion, and he would become the unofficial head of it.

Writer and historian Simon Schama referred to this as nothing short of "the recapture of the state's monopoly of authorized violence." And that was precisely what the Committee of Public Safety sought to achieve. Ever since the toppling of the Ancien Régime and the fall of the king, just about all respect for state-sanctioned authority had been lost. The old regime had been dismantled, and there was no longer any respect for the old authority.

The Committee of Public Safety was attempting to assert itself as the new authority and the only legitimate government body to inflict state-sanctioned pain, suffering, and death on the populace if the committee members deemed it necessary to do so. Nation states must have law and order. But the nature of that law and order depends on who is pulling the levers of power.

If proper checks and balances are put into place, there should be some sense of justice and fairness involved in how law and order and the coercive measures of the state are applied. But if you have just a dozen or so cronies who have questionable intentions, motives, political persuasions, and objectives at the wheel, anything could happen. And that was precisely what happened in France.

Nevertheless, the committee knew that to become the supreme French authority, they had to deal with the murderous mobs the revolution had created. It was their job to roll back the very monsters they had created. And it is here that we see the first signs of a decisive split between the French intelligentsia and the protesters in the street.

These two combined elements had supplied the basic formula for the French Revolution in the first place. The intelligentsia provided the brains, and the violent mobs in the streets provided the brawn. This deadly combination, which had rioters with bread and bloody heads on pikes chanting the slogans of political pamphlets that had been written by the intelligentsia, brought the Ancien Régime to its knees.

But now, the intelligentsia was turning its gaze on the rebels in the street. The first sign that this change was in the works occurred the previous February, in 1792, when rioters, infuriated with rising prices at shops, stormed the markets. They did not always steal outright. Many of them actually paid what they thought were fair prices. However, these rioters had no idea that the shopkeepers were just as much a victim of high prices as they were.

The shopkeepers had to deal with the inflated prices of the wholesalers from whom they got their goods. And the fact that these rioters were paying the shopkeepers just a fraction of the inflated prices they had posted meant that the shopkeepers lost money and faced the risk of going out of business. The leading lights of the revolution knew the rioters were making things worse. Maximilien Robespierre was infuriated by the actions of the protesters, especially since their main concern was over what he derisively referred to as mere "paltry merchandise." The fact that he would dismiss the need of the hungry like this is a clear indication that Robespierre did not really care about the suffering of the French people. The starving masses just wanted bread to feed their families. This was not merely a desire for paltry merchandise—it was a desire for survival during extraordinarily difficult times.

Robespierre had no patience for the day-to-day concerns of the protesters in the street. He desired a complete overhaul of French society more than anything else. Many of the people who looted stores just wanted the price of bread to go down. They could have cared less about many of the "ideals" promoted by Robespierre and his ilk. They just wanted food to eat.

The intellectuals had once used their fury over high prices to get the masses to do their bidding. However, once the Ancien Régime had been undone, the intelligentsia could care less about petty concerns over—as Robespierre put it—paltry merchandise. And so, as previously mentioned, a committee was formed to help stop the protests over high prices, the very thing that had sparked the revolution in the first place. Those who really gave it any thought must have realized how ridiculous and absurd all of this was.

It was as absurd as it was duplicitous. The same intellectuals who were more than willing to bring down the hammer on the peasants were the same ones who had fanned the flames of revolution in the years prior. When the king and queen were in charge, pamphlet after pamphlet was gleefully fired off the presses, accusing shopkeepers and the Ancien Régime of price gouging or even a grand conspiracy to purposefully inflict famine.

It was all well in good to make such gross lies and exaggerations to ignite violence from the masses when the king was in charge, but when the revolutionaries were on top, they readily dispensed with nonsense about price gouging and plots since they knew that it was their own bottom line that was at stake. They knew that it was not price gouging that was causing the dire economic condition but rather rampant and out-of-control inflation.

The revolutionaries further realized they were no better prepared to fix the troubled economy than the Ancien Régime had been. But even so, they wanted the protesters to keep quiet and were prepared to muster all of the forces at their disposal to silence them. The irony of their situation was not entirely lost on the leading intellectual figures of the revolution, though.

Perhaps revolutionary figure and firebrand Louis Antoine Léon de Saint-Just summed it up best when he spoke of how "misery had given birth to the revolution" and that "misery could destroy it." It was decided that the passions that sparked the French Revolution—the very passions the intelligentsia had inflamed—needed to be extinguished.

Chapter 5: The Revolutionary Wars Heat Up

"The Revolution had been prepared by the most civilized classes of the nation and carried out by the most uncivilized and the roughest of people."

-Alexis de Tocqueville

The threat of outside intervention had been looming for some time. France had spent the better part of several years as a former monarchy rapidly unraveling into chaos. As much as the British might have initially looked upon the misfortune of their French rivals with glee, they were growing increasingly concerned, as were the Austrians.

As mentioned, French Queen Marie Antoinette hailed from Austrian royalty. The Austrian emperor, Leopold II, was her brother. Leopold II was concerned but cautious when it came to conflicts with France. However, after his abrupt passing, his son Francis, who succeeded him, proved to be much bolder.

It is debated whether or not this boldness can be attributed to Francis or his handlers. Scholars have argued that it was the advisers of the new monarch who pushed for war more than Francis did. And these advisers were supposedly emboldened further since they were receiving regular updates on French troop positions through regular correspondence with Marie Antoinette.

Yes, by the time the queen was put on trial for treason, there was some indication that the charges might have had some truth. But even so, one can't help but sympathize with the queen. Her husband had been killed, and she was being held as a prisoner by revolutionary forces. Who can blame her for trying to solicit aid from her family in Austria?

With this backdrop of political power play in place, the War of the First Coalition took shape. Initially, France appeared to be in quite a bit of trouble. On September 2nd, 1793, the French fleet was forced to surrender to British forces at the port city of Toulon. This was a stunning blow. France had an army but did not have a proper fleet.

The deficiencies of the French navy would be a lasting problem throughout the revolution, as well as the future Napoleonic Wars. The port city would be recaptured on December 15th, 1793, by General Napoleon Bonaparte himself. Napoleon was just twenty-four years old at the time, yet he was already a rising star in the French military. His efforts were indeed noted, and he was subsequently put in charge of the French artillery.

Napoleon next took part in a siege of British positions at Toulon's Fort de l'Eguillette. During this exchange, the daring young Napoleon put himself in harm's way time and time again. In one instance, a cannonball soared right past him. Although he was not hit, it was so close that the force of it zooming past him caused him to fall as if he had been struck. One can only imagine the astonishment of those under his charge to see Bonaparte jumping right back up after this near miss to take charge of his troops.

At the end of the day, Napoleon and his troops were able to storm the fortress and raise the French flag over Toulon once again. Napoleon also ingratiated himself with the Robespierres, getting well acquainted with Maximilien's brother Augustin in particular. But it was small consolation in the aftermath of the smashed French fleet, which was destroyed on December 18th, 1793.

As bad as this blow was, the French authorities received another internal one when the incredibly miserable and starving French peasantry appeared en masse at the Hôtel de Ville of Paris in September 1793, shouting their old familiar cry of "Bread! Bread! We need bread!"

One can almost imagine the distressing sight of this poor, starving, and entirely uninformed rabble dressed in rags and chanting almost zombie-like for something to eat. Such a situation could not be ignored. An authority of the French commune of Paris, Pierre Gaspard "Anaxagoras" Chaumette, sought to calm the frayed nerves of the populace by announcing that price controls would be put in place to lower the price of bread by the end of the week.

However, the people were not having it, and the protesters refused to disperse, demanding an immediate solution to the scarcity that they faced. Pierre Chaumette then attempted to position himself in a more sympathetic light, shouting out to those assembled, "Well, I too have been poor, and as a result, I know what it is to be poor! This is an open war of the rich against the poor; they want to crush us; well, we must prevent them. We must crush them ourselves; we have the strength to do so!"

Once again creating an imaginary enemy out of "the rich," Pierre Chaumette took a tactic out of the revolutionary playbook. Chaumette was well known for his attempts to create enemies where there were none. Just prior to King Louis XVI's execution, he famously declared that much of the problems the French faced were simply because the king was still alive, as if the mere fact that the monarch was still breathing was the sole reason for inflation, internal unrest, and the war clouds that loomed on the horizon.

But even with the king dead, the likes of Chaumette were still searching for enemies they could blame France's problems on. After bantering back and forth with the crowd in this manner, it was then suggested that the protesters return the following day on September 5th, when the National Convention next convened, so they could speak openly of their grievances.

The demonstrators decided to do that, and like clockwork, they appeared at the National Convention as suggested. But they were not going to wait for the speeches of delegates to wrap up. Instead, they barged right into the hall and began using brute force against those whom they were told were holding out on them. The Jacobins, who reigned supreme, were ready, though. With a newly retooled *armée révolutionnaire* ("army of the revolution"), they put down the demonstrators and instituted a crackdown that would become known as the Reign of Terror.

Chapter 6: A Revolutionary Terror in Their Midst

"You who sustain the vacillating country against the torrent of despotism and intrigue, you whom I know as I know God by your miracles, I address myself to you, monsieur, to beg you to join with me in saving my poor region. I don't know you but you are a great man. You are not merely the deputy of a province; you are the representative of humanity and the republic."

-Louis Antoine Saint-Just

The start of the so-called "Reign of Terror" would leave countless dead and imprisoned. Although some scholars disagree on the start date of the Reign of Terror, most agree that it began with a Jacobin-inspired crackdown that was instituted on September 5th, 1793. Although no one knows the exact number, historians estimate that tens of thousands perished during this terrible episode in French history.

Its end can be definitively stated since it is generally agreed that it came to an end when its architect, Maximilien Robespierre, and his cronies became its last victims. Robespierre faced his own execution on July 28th, 1794. But a whole lot occurred in those nearly eleven fateful months of oppression. The first major milestone was when the Law of Suspects was issued on September 29th, 1793.

This legislation set down the exact procedures for rooting out supposed enemies of the state into French law. This set in motion a nationwide program of surveillance in which anyone who was deemed to be subversive was rounded up and arrested. Yes, ironically enough, as much as pre-revolutionary French philosophers had railed against the Spanish, Portuguese, and Roman inquisitions, the successors of the French Revolution decided it was high time to institute one of their own.

It is said that during this period, hundreds of thousands—some estimate roughly around 500,000—were placed under arrest. The fact that anyone could be arrested for just about any reason was an obvious departure from the supposed lofty goals of the French Revolution and the freedoms that were explicitly mentioned in the Declaration of the Rights of Man and of the Citizen.

Nevertheless, Jacobin leader Maximilien Robespierre had no problem with using force to secure his vision of France's future. He had no qualms about hauling supposed suspects before tribunals on the flimsiest of charges. As Robespierre himself put it at the time, "Public notoriety accuses a citizen of crimes of which no written proofs exist, but whose proof is in the heart of all indignant citizens."

What does that mean? Robespierre, with his chillingly cryptic words, is basically stating that there does not need to be any real, legal proof that a crime exists as long as someone has been deemed to be at odds with the heart of the revolution. If a person was believed to be subversive to the ideals of the revolution, they could expect wrath that poured from, as Robespierre put it, "the heart of all indignant citizens."

It truly is a chilling thing to contemplate. The Reign of Terror began as a coercive crackdown against riotous protests over the price of bread. However, most of those rounded up during this period were suspected of directly plotting against the revolutionary government. Religion sometimes played a role since Christianity was actively suppressed. Christianity came to be viewed as being potentially subversive, so outward showings of one's faith could land one into a lot of trouble with the revolutionaries. According to writer and historian Ian Davidson, if one was caught openly displaying a crucifix, they could be hauled in for questioning.

French society saw the complete breakdown of trust between friends and neighbors. As is always the case, when society is forced to look inward for "enemies," friends, neighbors, and even family members begin to turn against each other, with old grievances being settled under the guise of something larger than themselves. In the case of France in the 1790s, that larger thing was revolutionary fervor.

Esteemed French scholar and historian Jules Michelet openly admitted the Jacobins were the "thought police of the revolution." As Michelet put it, "It was not a small matter to be excluded from the Jacobins. This formidable society, while keeping the form of a club, was in reality a grand jury of accusers. Its membership list was the book of life or death."

One person who most certainly did not fit into this revolutionary club was the former French queen, Marie Antoinette. Perhaps the most hated focal point of the revolution, she managed to outlive her husband, who had been executed by way of the guillotine in January 1793. However, Marie's life would not last for long, as the thought police of the revolution found a way to bring her down as well. Immediately after her husband was killed, Marie Antoinette was placed under guard at the prison palace of the Temple.

It was hoped that the former French queen could remain out of sight and out of mind as far as the French people were concerned. However, during the summer of 1793, her handlers were shocked to find that word had been spreading of how tenderly the queen had been treating her two children—her surviving daughter and son—from their quarters in the Temple.

As absurd as it might sound, Marie Antoinette's handlers became alarmed that their dehumanization of the former royal would backfire. They feared that if the news became widespread, with people gossiping in the street that the queen was a caring and selfless mother, all of the great pains taken to paint her as a terrible monster might amount to nothing. After all, it is hard to vilify a person who is kind.

To stop the gossip from continuing, Marie Antoinette's seven-year-old son, Louis Charles, was ripped from her side. The boy was transferred to a cell below the queen's quarters, where she could hear his wretched sobs but do absolutely nothing to comfort him. Poor Louis would perish, locked away in his room, in 1795. He would have been only ten years old.

Marie Antoinette was ultimately hauled before the tribunal on October 14th, 1793. She was—predictably enough—tried for treason. She had much of the same old, recycled charges leveled at her, which used her ancestral roots to Austria to suggest that she was in cahoots with the Austrian government, with whom France was currently at war.

Despite the gravity of the situation and considering what she had already been through with the execution of her husband and all of the other deprivations that had been foisted upon her, she handled herself well. She denied her enemies the pleasure of seeing her grovel before them, as it is said that she stood tall and answered all the questions given to her with a firm and confident tone of voice.

She denied any wrongdoing and insisted that the happiness of the French people was always her and her husband's number one goal. Nevertheless, she was found guilty and would ultimately lose her head by way of the guillotine on October 16th, 1793. The morning prior to her execution, Marie Antoinette managed to write one last note to her sister-in-law Elisabeth.

The letter begins:

"It is to you, my sister, that I write for the last time. I have just been condemned, not a shameful death, for such is only for criminals, but to go and rejoin your brother."

The condemned queen is, of course, referring to her husband, who had already been guillotined. She reminds her sister-in-law Elisabeth that no matter what anyone might say, she could see through the condemnation that has been heaped upon them. Even though the two royals received the harshest of penalties, she did not see herself and her husband as being the same as criminals worthy of a shameful death.

She goes on to further stress her stance by stating, "Innocent like him, I hope to show the same firmness in my last moments. I am calm, as one is when one's conscience reproaches one with nothing."

Here, the queen again insists that her conscience is clear. It is true that the queen was unfairly targeted from the very start of her reign, but the fact that she refuses to even acknowledge that any mistakes might have been made on the part of the royals is a departure from King Louis XVI's reaction. Although King Louis thought that he and his wife had been unfairly targeted and dehumanized by the intelligentsia, he was willing to acknowledge his past mistakes.

Marie Antoinette's greatest concern was always for her children, whom she knew would have to live the rest of their lives (no matter how short they might be) without either of their parents. It was to this end that she implored her sister-in-law, Elisabeth, "who out of love have sacrificed everything to be with us," to look after the welfare of her two surviving children.

Her son, as previously mentioned, perished in his prison cell in 1795. It is hard to know what troubles he faced, although it does seem he was treated with some respect. However, during his autopsy, his body had marks all over it, as if he had been beaten. Marie Antoinette's daughter, Marie-Thérèse, would survive the Reign of Terror. She was released from captivity on December 18th, 1795, and she headed to Vienna, where she knew she would be welcomed.

Marie Antoinette then goes on to add, "I have learned from the proceedings at my trial that my daughter was separated from you. Alas! Poor child; I do not venture to write to her; she would not receive my letter. I do not even know whether this will reach you."

The queen was right to assume this, as her final missive did not actually reach its target. Elisabeth never even knew the letter existed. She would be sentenced to death by the guillotine in May 1794.

Marie Antoinette's letter goes on, with the queen hoping that her surviving son and daughter would learn to support each other through the many sorrows, trials, and tribulations that they would likely face in the aftermath of her demise.

The doomed queen advised, "Let them, in short, both feel that, in whatever positions they may be placed, they will never be truly happy but through their union. Let them follow our example. In our own misfortunes how much comfort has our affection for one another afforded us! And, in times of happiness, we have enjoyed that doubly from being able to share it with a friend; and where can one find friends more tender and more united than in one's own family?"

In the letter, Queen Marie Antoinette then turns her attention toward her son. She asks Elisabeth to make sure that the child keeps his father in his memory but also warns against him having any notion of seeking out vengeance.

She writes, "Let my son never forget the last words of his father, which I repeat emphatically; let him never seek to avenge our deaths."

It is thought-provoking to consider these final few words of the queen. Here, she is strongly suggesting that her son should not seek any vengeance against her and her husband's persecutors. It is perhaps a bit difficult to get inside the mind of this condemned monarch, but one must wonder if she was envisioning a future in which the monarchy was restored and her son was at its head. Did she imagine her son sitting on the throne as an adult and contemplating how he would exact vengeance against those who had wronged his parents?

In some ways, due to the incessant negative portrayals of Marie Antoinette by her detractors and some of her own statements, it is hard to imagine her wishing such magnanimity upon those who persecuted her and her family. But in one of her last moments of life, she seemed to believe that her son should show mercy and restraint should he live to take power over France.

Perhaps Marie Antoinette was influenced by Christian teachings on mercy and forgiveness. But perhaps she was wise enough to know that a cycle of retribution would not bode well for any monarchy. And history would ultimately bear this out when the monarchy was later restored under Louis XVI's brother, Louis XVIII.

Louis XVIII found that it was best to forgive and forget the terrible trespasses that had occurred as quickly as possible. Just as Marie Antoinette had stated in her final letter, it seemed that the only way to get out of the terrible cycle of hatred, grievance, and retribution that France had found itself in was to forgive, forget, and move on as much as was feasibly possible.

We can't forget, of course, that in these final words of Marie Antoinette, we see not just the last words of a monarch but also the pleas of a worried mother. Although the stoic queen was resigned to her own fate, she was deeply distressed over what might happen to her children. We get some indication of family discord with the queen's son as she urges her sister-in-law to be patient with the child, who apparently had caused some previous distress.

Marie Antoinette ends her missive, saying, "Farewell, my good and tender sister. May this letter reach you. Think always of me; I embrace you with all my heart, as I do my poor dear children. My God, how heart-rending it is to leave them forever! Farewell! Farewell!"

The letter did not reach Elisabeth; instead, it was seized by the prosecutor, Antoine Quentin Fouquier-Tinville, and then stashed away with his personal belongings. Although the note did not reach its intended target, it became an unexpected treasure for historians later on, marking the last moments prior to the former queen of France's demise.

At any rate, shortly after these last few heartfelt words were penned, Marie Antoinette was marched to the guillotine to meet her untimely end. She was hauled out of her jail cell around seven in the morning and placed inside an open carriage (some describe it as more of a cart), where she was completely exposed to the elements, including anything the crowds might throw at her. To make matters worse, her transport was purposefully stopped on more than one occasion so that her handlers could point her out to the crowd.

During these moments, seething throngs of Marie Antoinette's former subjects mocked and hurled all kind of vile words and cruel taunts her way. Nevertheless, it is said that she remained stoic and strong and did not stoop to their level. Instead of shouting down the abusive mob, she was heard mouthing prayers to God. Although this was meant to be the execution of a former monarch, in many ways, Marie Antoinette took on the guise of a martyr.

The death of Marie Antoinette was just as dramatic as the saints of old being led to burn at the stake or being thrown to the lions. The procession to the guillotine was a major ordeal, and it was already the middle of the day by the time the former queen reached her destination. Stoic and refined until the end, it is said that her last words came about when she accidentally stepped on her executioner's foot. She was heard telling him, "Excuse me, sir, I did not do it on purpose."

It was as if Marie Antoinette was resigned to her fate and determined to stand in stark contrast to the bloodthirsty mob that howled for her demise. Unlike those who clamored for her death, she wanted to make it absolutely clear that she had no rancor within her. As the guillotine dropped, she remained quiet. And without any sign of protest, the life of the queen had been snuffed out.

Even more pivotal for the course of the revolution was what happened a couple of weeks later. On October 31ˢᵗ, twenty-one leaders of the disgraced and demobilized Girondins were executed. The pretense of any sense of justice was not even bothered with at this point. According to French historian Michelet, "There was no hypocrisy in the trial. Everybody saw right away that it was just about killing. They disregarded all formalities still customary at this period in the Tribunal revolutionaries. No documents were produced. There were no lawyers for the defense. Several of the accused were not allowed to speak."

The propaganda of the intellectual elite had fallen flat. Even the simplest of simpletons could see that the wool was being pulled over their eyes and that the elitists had blood on their hands. There was no way to sugarcoat the fact that blood lust was being engaged on an official level through the organs of the state.

Show trials are all about trotting folks out and publicly condemning them without any hope of recourse or defense. And that is what happened to these condemned former leaders of the Girondins. Yes, it was a grisly Halloween in 1793, as the last vestiges of the Girondins were ground under the heel of the Jacobin boot.

It is worth noting that the first French Constitution had already been scrapped at this point in favor of another constitution, which was partially drafted by the leading Jacobin architect of the Reign of Terror, Maximilien Robespierre. This new constitution was formally adopted in June of 1793. The supposed constitutional monarchy of the first constitution became null and void after the king lost his head. So, Robespierre's obvious impetus was to forge a constitution that did not have any need for a monarch to be involved.

Besides abrogating the need for the monarchy, the document also greatly expanded upon the original virtues declared in the Declaration of the Rights of Man and of the Citizen. In particular, it sought to ensure things like popular sovereignty, the right of association, and the right to resist oppression. The right to resist oppression was the vaguest of these supposed rights. Just how does one define oppression? And how could one say that they weren't being oppressed at the time? After all, the Reign of Terror was in full swing, with multiple fingers pointing in multiple directions at multiple oppressors, both real and imagined.

The Jacobin-backed Reign of Terror was so wide-reaching that by December of that year, more than fifty detention centers were in operation in Paris alone. And by that December, they contained some seventy thousand souls between them. The people who were arrested and executed included men and women, both rich and poor and obscure and prominent.

One of the highest-ranking prisoners was Louis Philippe II, Duke of Orléans. He was known to be the most affluent figure in all of France and had once been an elected representative in the National Convention. He was also a cousin of the former king, whom he had actually voted to have executed. Louis Philippe was arrested simply because his son proved treacherous to the revolutionary cause when he fled to enemy lines and switched sides.

His son—the Duke of Chartres—had become quite disgusted with his father when he voted to have King Louis XVI executed. Having had enough of the revolutionary fervor that gripped France, he decided to defect to the Austrians, taking up refuge with them and fighting for them. This would prove to be ironic since just prior to his son making this fateful decision, Louis Philippe II, Duke of Orleans, in his capacity as a representative of the National Convention, had voted to approve a protocol that stated anyone viewed to be even the slightest bit complicit with a defector became a suspect by default.

Louis Philippe II was found guilty by association, and that was more than enough for the revolution to suspect him. Louis Phillippe was known for having a great sense of humor, and he apparently took it all in stride. Noting the absurdity of it all, just prior to his execution, he is said to have remarked, "Really? This seems a bit of a joke."

However, not everyone was laughing. Some leading lights of the revolution did try and put the brakes on the Reign of Terror. For instance, on December 5th, 1793, Camille Desmoulins published a pamphlet called *Le Vieux Cordelier*, which called for an end to the persecution. In another issue that was released on December 17th, 1793, Camille Desmoulins was bold enough to directly call for an end to the Reign of Terror.

Robespierre initially took a surprisingly conciliatory tone to these attacks on the methodology of the Reign of Terror. On December 20th, he proposed to set up a committee of justice, which would reexamine some of those being held under suspicion. This conciliatory and tame response only emboldened Desmoulins further. In his next publication on December 24th, he demanded that the prisoners be immediately released.

He declared, "Unlock the prisons for the 200,000 citizens whom you call suspects, because, in the Declaration of Rights, there are no houses of suspicion. You want to exterminate all your enemies by the guillotine! But was there ever a greater madness? Believe me, liberty would be strengthened and Europe conquered if you had a Committee of Clemency!"

Still, Maximilien Robespierre showed unusual restraint when dealing with the fired-up Desmoulins. Robespierre even waved off the suggestion of expelling him from the Jacobin Club. Instead, he stated that he would merely destroy his publications. However, Robespierre's tolerance would not last forever, and Desmoulins, along with several other dissenters, were rounded up and arrested. Camille Desmoulins would be given a farce of a trial just prior to his execution on April 5th, 1794.

And shortly thereafter, the French Revolution did indeed devolve into what seemed to be complete and utter nonsense. In the spring of 1794, Robespierre, seeking to keep up the revolutionary fervor of the populace, began to create what can only be described as a religious cult. Ever since the beginning of the French Revolution, there were many who wished to dismantle Christianity and replace it with a new religion.

Many of the leading lights of the revolution were deists who believed in a higher power while having great disdain for organized religion. These sentiments were echoed in the fact that the French Constitution mentioned a "supreme being" but did not go as far as to specify what that supreme being might be. Robespierre felt the need to fill the void that the suppression of Christianity had created, so he began to create his own religion, placing himself at the head.

He led religious processions and had people sing their own improvised hymns in which they sang not praises to God but to the glories of the revolution and their detestation of monarchs. As ridiculous as it all sounds, there were plenty of poor, disillusioned French who fell into the cult.

Robespierre's colleagues were not pleased with these developments and secretly despised his efforts. Robespierre's cult was more a cult of personality than anything else, and as soon as he was dispatched, his experimental religion would fall by the wayside as well.

The Reign of Terror was running out of steam, and neither it nor a new religion for the masses would bolster the fortunes of Robespierre and his Jacobin colleagues.

Nevertheless, Robespierre sought to involve all aspects of the lives of the common French with his new cult. The culmination of all of this religion was an extravagant production that Robespierre put together on June 20th, which was referred to as the Festival of the Supreme Being.

During Robespierre's invocation at this event, he proclaimed, "The true priest of the Supreme Being is Nature itself; its temple is the universe; its religion virtue; its festivals the joy of a great people assembled under its eyes to tie the sweet knot of universal fraternity and to present before it [Nature] the homage of pure and feeling [sensible] hearts."

Using themes, symbolism, and words that he felt would resonate with the French people, Robespierre was trying to stir the hearts and minds of the masses. He was trying to get a reaction. But he did not expect the reaction that he ultimately received.

Chapter 7: The Thermidorian Reaction and the Directory

"It has been said that terror is the principle of despotic government. Does your government therefore resemble despotism? Yes, as the sword that gleams in the hands of heroes of liberty resembles that with which the henchmen of tyranny are armed. The government of the revolution is liberty's despotism against tyranny."

-Maximilien Robespierre

Robespierre desperately sought to transform the face of French society. He renamed the month of July as "Thermidor." And in the month of Thermidor, his opponents moved against him in what has been subsequently dubbed the "Thermidorian Reaction." The term "Thermidorian" is a historically vague one. Anyone who opposed Robespierre and the direction in which he was leading France fell into this catch-all category.

Some of the opposition were against Robespierre on a purely ideological level, while others might have had personal vendettas against Robespierre or were acting out of fear. Some who had gotten on Robespierre's bad side might have felt that taking out Robespierre would be the only way to avoid losing their own head.

On a very basic level, the Thermidorians were those who believed Robespierre had overstepped his bounds and were seeking to curtail the abuses that this enlightened madman had unleashed. As a result, Robespierre and his fellow Jacobins were thoroughly denounced.

Robespierre would be cornered, and during an attempt to arrest him, he would try his hand at suicide.

The effort failed, and he ended up with a shattered jaw instead. Robespierre was seized while in this terrible state and put on trial. One more sham trial later, and he would be marched off to the guillotine. The bandage covering his jaw was deemed to be too much of a distraction, so it was forcibly ripped off of him. And unless an animal howl of pain counts, Robespierre, the great orator, did not have any last words. He howled in pain, the blade went down, and he was gone.

However, the tumult was not yet over, and the Thermidorian Reaction would continue. Southern France, in particular, would see spontaneous eruptions of violence against Jacobins. One must realize that southern France was staunchly Catholic, and much of its reaction can be traced back to the way the Jacobins tried to suppress the Catholic Church.

Also, during this reactionary wave, former political opponents of Robespierre and the Jacobins were released from prison. The Girondins were put back in power. This led to a renewed spate of retribution, this time aimed at the Jacobins and their supporters. Some of this retribution was on the official level, with Jacobins being arrested and detained, but much of the rest of it took place in the streets in the form of spontaneous eruptions of reactionary, mob violence of the worst kind. After all, there were many scores to be settled.

The Thermidorians created even more trouble by removing the price controls the Jacobin administration had instituted to get the rising cost of food under control. This led to renewed shortages, and once again, the average French citizen was in a desperate state of affairs. Their desperation led to what has been cited as the last major protest of the French Revolution.

On May 20th, 1795, a huge mob of French protesters stormed into a political convention that was being held among the Thermidorians. Just prior to this protest, legislation was passed that gave representatives of the Thermidorian government sweeping authoritarian power, allowing them to arrest and disarm any rabble-rousers as they saw fit.

Dismissing any previous notions of the citizenry having the right to protest, the elites who wielded power had little time or pity for the commoners and used martial force to dispel and disperse them. In the aftermath of this dispersal, the Directory was created on June 21st, 1795.

The Thermidorian reactionaries were determined not to be swayed by the previous radical reforms of the Jacobins and insisted on a more conservative constitution.

The Directory was basically a legislative body made up of two houses: the Council of Ancients and the Council of 500. The Council of Ancients was the upper chamber, which had the authority to approve or reject legislation proposed by the lower chamber, known as the Council of 500. The Council of Ancients did not propose new legislation themselves, but it was up to its members to approve governmental reforms.

At the top of this structure was an executive branch, a board of five directors. These five directors consisted of well-known members of the revolutionary elite: Paul Barras, Louis Marie de La Révellière-Lépeaux, Jean-François Rewbell, Étienne-François-Louis-Honoré Letourneur, and Lazare Carnot.

The makeup of the Directory was fairly ingenious and had the potential for some much-needed checks and balances in the French legislature. Members were put in place through an indirect method of specially designated electors. The governing council was meant to be held accountable by the legislature.

It is important to note that as much as the French Revolution was inspired by the American Revolution, the major difference was that the American Founding Fathers focused on employing checks and balances between governmental bodies, whereas the French, with their political clubs routinely vying to monopolize all power, dangerously lacked any checks to prevent authoritarian abuse. Still, the Directory was just a fledgling enterprise at its outset and was in danger of dissolving from the beginning.

And from its very inception, there were plots and counterplots in the works between various political factions. One of the most infamous dissenters of the Directory was François-Noël Babeuf. Babeuf was known for his left-wing ideology and was a known agitator in France. He was briefly imprisoned in 1790, and upon his release, he began to work on a firebrand periodical to spread his views.

In the *Correspondant Picard*, Babeuf wrote about his ideas on agrarian reform. With echoes of the future ethos of communism, he insisted that there should be a general redistribution of land. Babeuf believed the wealth earned by others needed to be gathered up and redistributed to the masses. He disregarded the virtues of hard work and merit and sought to forcibly achieve economic equality through forcible redistribution.

At the height of the Reign of Terror, in the spring of 1793, Babeuf was once again arrested, only to be released in July 1794 after the architect of the terror, Robespierre, was arrested. Ironically, Babeuf came to prominence again during the reactionary wave of the Thermidorians. In the Thermidorians' mad rush to reverse course and undo everything the Jacobins had done, they practically dumped all of the prisoners arrested by the Jacobin regime onto the street.

But although Babeuf was no friend of the Jacobins, he would soon prove himself to be a thorn in the side of the Directory. After he began to openly deride the efforts of the Thermidorians, he was again placed into custody on February 12th, 1795. He would not stop, and even after he was released, he continued to make plans for overthrowing the Directory so that he could institute his own plans for the redistribution of wealth.

This time around, he was able to pull many disgruntled Jacobins into his orbit. With this new political coalition, Babeuf began speaking about a renewed push for revolution in November 1795. Babeuf's efforts would ultimately be defeated, and he would be again arrested in May 1796. This was ultimately the end of the road for Babeuf, who was subsequently tried for treason, found guilty, and executed the following year.

The driving force behind the Directory was a French general named Paul Barras. He was actually a close associate of Napoleon Bonaparte. Barras would open the door for Napoleon's eventual entrance into executive leadership.

Initially, the Directory did not fare well, and as the political body of France once again went into a fit of convulsions, France faced a wave of counterrevolutionary activity that threatened to pull the rug right out from under the Directory.

Coincidentally enough, Bonaparte and the troops at his command were able to prevent the Directory's complete collapse. As the general's compound was being targeted, Napoleon strategically positioned artillery around it to ensure that it was not stormed. Under Napoleon's watch, there would not be another storming of the Bastille. In fact, these efforts could be viewed as France's first steps in its long march toward authoritarianism.

But paradoxically enough, these efforts led to Napoleon being heralded as a savior of the republic. For his efforts, he was made the commander of the Army of the Interior. Napoleon essentially declared martial law and was able to go from house to house taking weapons. Since the revolution and unrest had begun with the storming of the Bastille and the seizure of arms, Napoleon realized that the only way to have order would be to take those arms back.

Interestingly enough, while he was in the midst of this search, he met a kid named Eugène de Beauharnais. One of Napoleon's men was attempting to take a sword from twelve-year-old Eugène, but the child begged him not to take it since it had belonged to his deceased father. The young man confronted Napoleon and declared that he would end his own life if the sword was not returned at once.

Napoleon felt sorry for this kid and relented. Despite his own instructions to seize all weapons, he made an exception for Eugène. Napoleon would meet the boy's mother, Joséphine, a short time later, and the two would almost immediately hit it off. Joséphine would become Napoleon's first wife, with the two becoming wed on March 9th, 1796. Although Napoleon was not a central figure in the French Revolution at its beginning, he would take a leading role later.

From the perspective of France's foes, their main objective was to contain the turmoil of France and make sure its problems did not spill over into neighboring regions. For Austria, its role and objectives were far more personal. The queen of France, who hailed from Austrian royalty, had been executed. Austria was also in steep debt due to the War of the First Coalition.

Austria was more determined than other nations to settle the score with France. Austria had technically been at war with France ever since 1792, and it was the one with the most to lose should it fail. And it was determined to come out on top. Ever since hostilities had erupted in that fateful year of 1792, the disputed Piedmont region of northern Italy had served as the main battleground. Napoleon rolled the dice by throwing the vast bulk of his troops at the Austrian armies encamped in Piedmont near the Alpine region of France.

Initially, it seemed as if the French were destined to lose. Beaten and battered from previous conflicts, they were almost entirely unprepared. There was a dire lack of equipment, and many of the French troops lacked proper footwear, trekking the snowy mountains practically barefoot.

Napoleon addressed these needs just prior to the battle. Bonaparte is said to have proclaimed, "Soldiers, you are insufficiently clothed, malnourished; the government owes you much but is unable to repay anything. I wish to lead you into the most fertile valleys of the world. Wealthy regions, large cities will be under your power. You will find in those parts honor, glory, and riches." His troops rallied and were sent hurtling into the Alps to face the Austrians.

The first battle commenced on April 12th, 1796, when French forces faced off against tens of thousands of Austrian soldiers. Napoleon was able to lead his troops to a soaring victory. Within a matter of moments, French artillery mowed down the Austrians. Thousands of Austrian troops perished in the first few rounds of fighting in the Battle of Montenotte. This battle would leave thousands of Austrians dead, and eventually, the Austrian forces were forced to make a hasty retreat.

It would take about a month of continued sustained losses, but the Austrians ultimately were driven out of Piedmont. It was a stunning success, and Napoleon was not afraid to boast of his achievement. After the Austrians were driven out, he declared, "Soldiers! In fifteen days, you have gained six victories, taken twenty-one colors and 55 pieces of artillery, seized several fortresses and conquered the richest parts of Piedmont."

And soon after, Napoleon would chase the Austrians all the way to Vienna. At this point, the Austrian emperor was forced to sue for peace. The subsequent peace talks led to the Treaty of Campo Formio.

This treaty was a great boon for France since it resulted in the French taking control of Piedmont and Lombardy (northern Italy). The French were also given control of the western bank of the Rhineland. However, it would not be long before France's foes would recalibrate and form a new coalition.

Chapter 8: The War of the Second Coalition and the Rise of Napoleon

"The battlefield is a scene of constant chaos. The winner will be the one who controls that chaos, both his own and the enemies."

-Napoleon Bonaparte

After Austria made peace with France, Britain had to fight the French alone. Nevertheless, the Austrians and the French continued to have issues with each other. There were still arguments over territorial disputes, and Austria was concerned about continued French warfare in other regions. In the summer of 1798, the French launched a sudden invasion of Egypt and Syria.

Napoleon shocked the world with this feat, as it seemed to come entirely out of left field. However, the move actually made a lot of sense. The French were not in a position to invade Britain as they would have liked due to insufficient naval strength to launch a cross-Channel invasion. But much of Britain's wealth at this time was due to its territorial possessions and trade networks that had been established through Egypt and onward all the way to India. In other words, the French were on a mission to cut off this valuable supply route.

Before getting to the coasts of North Africa, Napoleon Bonaparte's forces would make a pitstop at the island of Malta. Here, the French forces besieged an order of knights known as the Hospitallers. The

Hospitallers, who had their origins in the Crusades, had spent the past few centuries fending off Islamic incursions. Yet Napoleon was able to do what previous invading armies could not—he successfully laid siege to and overran the knights' fortifications. After just one day of fighting, the knights raised the white flag and handed over the island to Napoleon Bonaparte. The French now had the perfect weigh station to use on their way to Egypt.

The French ousting of the Hospitallers managed to incur the wrath of Russian Tsar Paul I. The Russian tsar had close ties with the knights and had been made an honorary "protector of the order" just prior to Napoleon's takeover of Malta. However, Russia was not about to declare war on France; instead, it sat on the sidelines to see how things would play out.

Egypt has shifted hands multiple times over the millennia. Of course, Egypt was the land of the pharaohs, who commissioned the building of the pyramids. The pharaohs were toppled by the armies of Alexander the Great. Egypt was made part of a Greek empire before it was seized by Rome, where it spent several centuries as the bread basket of the Roman Republic and then the Roman Empire. The Romans lost Egypt when Islamic armies swept down into the Middle East and North Africa.

The language of Egypt became Arabic, and its religion became Islam. Egypt would be administered by a wide range of Islamic dynasties, with one of those later dynasties being the Ottoman Empire. By the time of Napoleon's invasion, the Ottomans were in decline, and their grip on Egypt was weak. Egypt was essentially autonomous, being run by an Egyptian/Arabic group called the Mamluks.

Napoleon knew this. Part of his scheme was to defeat the Mamluks and then hand Egypt back to the Ottomans to curry the favor of the sultan. However, his plan had a fatal flaw since the sultan in faraway Turkey did not see the situation the same way Napoleon did. The Ottomans still considered Egypt theirs, and as soon as Napoleon and his troops landed, their actions were considered an act of war.

The French forces arrived in Egypt on June 30th, 1798. The landing was fraught with challenges. Napoleon had thousands of troops on foreign soil attempting to maneuver heavy artillery equipment in uncertain conditions. It certainly was not an easy task, but Napoleon was a man who liked a challenge. Napoleon and his army struggled onward and managed to reach the gates of Alexandria on July 2nd.

After a struggle, they seized a fortress situated right along the city walls. Napoleon then had a translator compile a written statement, which was delivered to the citizens of the city. The statement read, "People of Egypt. I come to restore your rights, to punish the usurpers; I respect God, his prophet and the Quran more than did the Mamluks. We are the friends of all true Muslims."

But the Egyptians were not so easily convinced. They took one look at these foreigners and decided they were not the friendly "liberators" they were claiming to be. Thus, the Egyptians continued to resist the French advance. As the French attempted to enter the city, they found they would have to battle practically the whole populace.

However, the outdated muskets used by the city's defenders were no match for Napoleon's cutting-edge artillery, giving the French a decisive advantage. Napoleon's forces were able to slice right through a desperate cavalry charge with punishing rounds of artillery. Alexandria was soon Napoleon's.

Britain responded to Napoleon's actions too late, but it still had a trick up its sleeve. The French fleet had already been battered by the British; Napoleon had taken what was left of it to make the trip to Egypt. In his haste to get to Alexandria, he left the craft unprotected. The British took advantage of this, sending its navy to bombard the French fleet. The ships were completely destroyed. Napoleon and his army were now marooned in Egypt.

Napoleon knew there was no turning back, so he went on the offensive and charged into Cairo. On July 21st, he launched what became known as the Battle of the Pyramids.

During this battle, Napoleon and his army faced off against an Egyptian Mamluk commander named Murad Bey. This exchange ended up turning out much like the battle in Alexandria. The Mamluk army was decimated, and Napoleon marched into Cairo on July 24th, 1798.

As successful as Napoleon was, there was a strong coalition forming against him. In fact, it was the formation of a second coalition, and it would lead to the War of the Second Coalition.

The coalition that waged this war against France took some time to form. The first step was when Naples allied itself with Austria, with the two joining forces on May 19th, 1798. The next major step was when Russia allied itself with Naples on November 29th. Shortly thereafter, the Austrian chancellor Johann Amadeus von Thugut attempted to bring the

Prussians on board, but his efforts ultimately came to nothing.

Austria and Britain were not able to achieve a formal alliance, but they would unofficially cooperate in what has been termed "ad hoc cooperation." As these official and unofficial alliances were coming together, the next major piece of the puzzle was put in place when the Russians allied themselves with the Ottoman Empire on December 23rd and then with the British on December 26th of that fateful year of 1798.

One of the first major engagements of the coalition forces occurred the following year, in the summer of 1799, when a British/Russian force fought its way into the Netherlands. They battled the French and the Dutch forces that had aligned with them. The British and Russian forces were forced to retreat from the Netherlands after they were stymied by French forces in the Battle of Castricum on October 6th, 1799. Ultimately, the French and Dutch positions were too formidable, and the British/Russian troops were forced to retreat.

In the meantime, Napoleon had left Egypt for Gaza, where he defeated a strategic garrison at the city el-Arish. The French battled their way up the coast to the heavily fortified city of Acre. However, this Middle Eastern fortress proved to be too formidable, and Napoleon ended up retreating to Egypt. He arrived just in time to greet a British/Turkish army, which disembarked on July 11th.

The Turks managed to take the city of Aboukir, but a retooled French army led by Napoleon charged right into their positions. Thanks to the use of heavy artillery, the French were able to decimate their opponents. After this latest victory, Napoleon left his subordinates to sort out the administration of Egypt while he returned to France that October. He returned to bear witness to the latest problems in the body politic of France.

Since the eruption of new wide-ranging hostilities, the Directory instituted a highly unpopular draft, which forced men between the ages of twenty and twenty-five to enlist. Draft resistance was quite common, and troops often frequently deserted after being called to service. Morale was even lower when it was realized that the troops that did decide to fight would not be properly equipped due to a lack of proper goods.

Many blamed the French government's inability to properly equip its troops on deep-seated corruption in the Directory. All of this discontent led to yet another spate of political upheaval on June 18th, 1799, as four of the five directors of the Directory were ousted. Their replacements were considered "conservatives" and "revisionists" who wished to roll back the French Revolution to restore the rights that had been promised back in 1789.

It is worth noting that although the rights promised in 1789, such as the right to free speech, were considered liberal back in the days of the Tennis Court Oath, France had been through so much revolutionary turmoil that these basic rights were considered conservative. Although it might be hard to grasp, it does make some sense. The radical tenants of Maximilian Robespierre, which had led to the Reign of Terror and ultimately the Thermidorian Reaction, seemed far more revolutionary than the rights promised back in 1789.

However, there were still those who wanted more. People felt that the rights enshrined in the French Constitution did not go far enough. A very vocal group of Neo-Jacobins insisted that the newer variations of the French Constitution should stand and harangued the conservatives as being nothing short of "oligarchs." Napoleon waltzed right into this fray, and the conservative faction, seeking military support, sought his martial strength to put down their rivals.

They might have sought his help, but Bonaparte ultimately overthrew the Directory and took power himself. Napoleon and his troops launched a coup on November 9th, 1799. Bonaparte ordered that the current constitution be discarded in favor of drafting a new one. Bonaparte was placed in a position to oversee all of these changes as the first consul. Although he was not yet calling himself emperor, the position of first consul essentially gave Napoleon final authority over all matters of governance. This coup is typically seen as the end of the French Revolution, as Napoleon would bring some stability to the country.

Napoleon continued to lead the troops. In early June, the French were able to seize Milan and then a whole string of towns, such as Pavia, Piacenza, Stradella, and other parts of the Lombardy region. This effectively cut off the Austrian supply lines heading east along the banks of the Po River. The French then collided with the Austrian army in the vicinity of Marengo on June 14th. The French numbered around twenty-eight thousand, while the Austrians were thirty thousand strong. Along with a numerical advantage, the Austrians also had better artillery.

But the fighting spirit was with the French, and they were able to completely drive the Austrians from Italy. This victory not only solidified

French positions in Italy but also Napoleon Bonaparte's position in the French government. The conquering hero Napoleon (at least for the moment) could do no wrong.

It was just a brief walk to outright absolutism, with Napoleon being made consul for life in 1802 and then the emperor of France in 1804. It was also declared that the imperial mantle would carry on as a hereditary title through Napoleon's offspring. Yes, after several years of terrible bloodshed in which the French monarchy had been overthrown, the French found themselves back at square one by instituting a new absolute monarchy.

Ever since the 1791 constitution, the French government had experimented with representative republicanism, which ultimately led to the Directory and its bicameral legislature. However, all of these efforts were stopped in their tracks when Napoleon took over. Until Napoleon was overthrown, all legislature would be executive in nature, and it would be enacted at the dictatorial whims of Napoleon Bonaparte.

Although Napoleon later became the emperor of France, it is very important to make note of the fact that Napoleon was a major promoter of the ideals of the Enlightenment. Yes, he was a despot, but he was an enlightened despot. Also, Napoleon Bonaparte stands out as a clear indication that history and its principal characters are far more complicated than we typically give them credit. Napoleon might have ruled with an iron fist, but he also ensured that many of the basic freedoms espoused by the great minds of the Enlightenment were put in place.

In a strange twist, Napoleon, a man whose own personal morality many might have questioned even then, had been placed as the gatekeeper of morality in France. He arrived when France was at a juncture between anarchy and chaos, and it was suddenly up to him to ensure that the basic personal freedoms gained by the French were not lost. So, he had to use the powers at his disposal to keep that from happening, even though those powers were more of an absolute monarch than a representative government.

Under Napoleon, a person was free (at least for the most part) in France, but that freedom had limits. People weren't free to randomly attack, rob, and brutalize those they did not like, but they were free to have their own basic rights as long as they did not interfere with others. And just like the former rights that were espoused by the Enlightenment, these freedoms only affected men, not women. Also, as time passed, Napoleon reinstated slavery, which had been banned by the French government in 1795.

Still, in many ways, the basic freedoms that Napoleon enforced created the much-needed balance of basic liberties and a clear and stable legal framework. The Napoleonic Code outlined the people's freedoms while simultaneously ensuring that those freedoms would not get out of hand as they had during the French Revolution. The Napoleonic Code established clear and concise guidelines that could not be altered at the mere whim of passionate mobs, biased judges, or other unforeseen events.

In contrast to the shifting sands of the Reign of Terror, which had been brought on by the French Revolution and stirred up all manner of wild accusations, trumped-up charges, and mob rule, Napoleon's new legal framework would not be swayed by rumors and gossip. The Napoleonic Code was put in place as a solid bulwark upon which society could rest.

The Napoleonic Code was so stable that its legacy continues to be a major part of French society to this very day. So, yes, Napoleon was a dictator and caused all kinds of war and turmoil in multiple countries during the course of his many military adventures. But we also must give credit where credit is due. And we must acknowledge the legal stability that was established during Napoleon Bonaparte's time in power.

Conclusion: The Lasting Impact of the French Revolution

The French Revolution was an impactful event in France and world history. Although the French Revolution was sparked to answer a major dilemma facing the French people, its ramifications ended up affecting the whole world.

Much has been said about how many of the ideals and actions of the French Revolution inspired other global movements, but let's take a look at a movement that often gets overlooked in favor of the Latin American independence wars, for example. Karl Marx was inspired by the French commune of Paris.

The notion that the common man of the street could shake off an entrenched power like the French monarchy has left a lasting legacy. And those who wished to do likewise in other parts of the world would look toward the French Revolution as both an example and an inspiration.

Despite all of the bloodshed, terror, and repercussions, the French Revolution stood out as some sort of beacon of hope. After all, the French Revolution overturned the normal state of affairs and allowed the common person to voice their grievances. It was only in the later stages of the revolution that this spirit was lost, as the Jacobins and others among the revolutionary elite wished to crack down and solidify their gains. This tyrannical maneuver has been widely repeated by oppressive tyrants and regimes that have come on the heels of bloody revolutions.

Lenin and Stalin promised the same kind of utopian freedoms to their people as the French did. And just like Robespierre at his worst, they decided to dispatch with the revolutionaries once they had served their purpose.

The intellectual elites felt they knew how to fashion society better than anyone else. They were seeking to recreate civilization (and even spirituality) in their own image. Nothing captures the height of this hubris than Robespierre's "cult of the Supreme Being." Even his colleagues could not help but balk at these shenanigans. And if he had not been stopped, it is quite possible that he might have achieved his aim of creating a religion with himself as its head.

The executions and persecution during the French Revolution, something that were seen as "civil" solutions to social problems at the time, would be latched onto and repeated by the most despicable political movements. The French chose to kill enemies of the state by way of guillotine because they viewed this instrument as a humane way to fix the social ills that plagued France.

This was the same sentiment expressed by the Nazis, who opted to create elaborate gas chambers to kill those whom they deemed "undesirable." Nazi bureaucrats, such as Joseph Goebbels and Heinrich Himmler, were notorious paper pushers who recoiled at the mere sight of blood, yet they were okay with authorizing the deaths of millions by way of gas.

In much the same way, the French revolutionaries felt the guillotine was a humane way to kill others. This belief was actually professed by this instrument of the Reign of Terror's namesake, Dr. Joseph-Ignace Guillotin. He declared that this device of death, which ultimately took his own name, the guillotine, was the best means to ensure his own "philanthropic" sense of humanitarianism.

To be fair to Dr. Guillotin, he most certainly never dreamed that this instrument of death would be used for large-scale indiscriminate killing. Guillotin was more likely envisioning this tool of execution to be the last resort and used to execute condemned criminals in a humane way. Before the guillotine, people were subjected to horrendous torture and cruel deaths. For instance, the breaking wheel was a popular form of public execution. A criminal would be tied to the floor and then have his bones broken by way of this large, heavy wheel, which sometimes had spikes on it. The wheel would be dropped on the body again and again, crushing the bones of its victims. Next, the criminal would be strapped to the wheel and placed on a pole. The executioner would then decapitate or strangle the accused to death. Sometimes, a criminal would be strapped to the wheel and thrown into a fire. Even a typical beheading, a form of execution that was reserved for the nobility, often took more than one try to decapitate the accused, leading to cries of agony instead of a swift death.

The breaking wheel would be abolished in 1791, but it was just one of many excruciating punishments from this time. In light of this, it makes sense that men like Guillotin sought a humane way to get rid of criminals who could not be reformed. Guillotin actually sought to end capital punishment, but he was not successful. So, he instead sought a means to humanely put those guilty of murder, brutal assault, and the most heinous of crimes to death. Dr. Guillotin likely did not foresee the guillotine being used to silence political opposition on a massive scale.

Unlike Guillotin, the French revolutionaries who readily employed the guillotine did not hesitate to use the guillotine as their means of crushing their opponents. They believed that with the quick pull of a cord and the hissing of a blade, political opponents could be silenced quickly without much effort or having to hear their cries for very long. The killing was easy. Today, we would liken it to pushing a button to get rid of someone. The ease with which people were killed via the guillotine helped to desensitize the executioners and those ordering the executions.

After the fall of Robespierre, Napoleon Bonaparte came along and brought some sanity back to French society. It is true that he was a military dictator, but he did bring back a sense of normalcy with his Napoleonic Code. He also restored the church. Although Napoleon was not particularly devout, he probably figured that if people needed religion, they might as well keep the one they were familiar with instead of creating a brand new one.

Napoleon would ultimately be deposed, and the French would face more problems. There was a brief return to the constitutional monarchy until the rise of Napoleon III, the nephew of the original imperial upstart. It was only after the fall of Napoleon III that France took on its more familiar shape of a modern-day republic, with senators and a sitting president at its head.

France has been through quite a few twists and turns in history, and the whole world has been affected as a consequence. To this very day, the French Revolution still stands as one of the starkest examples of both the best and worst of humanity. The French Revolution brought us the Rights of Man and of the Citizen but also the "terror" of the guillotine. Great intellectual thought and discourse were matched by the unreasoning belligerence of mobs. The French Revolution was a perplexing paradox that both intrigues and haunts us to this very day.

Here's another book by Enthralling History that you might like

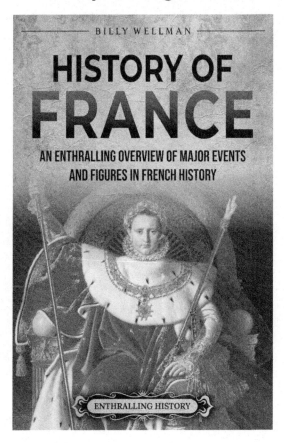

Free limited time bonus

Stop for a moment. We have a free bonus set up for you. The problem is this: we forget 90% of everything that we read after 7 days. Crazy fact, right? Here's the solution: we've created a printable, 1-page pdf summary for this book that you're reading now. All you have to do to get your free pdf summary is to go to the following website:

https://livetolearn.lpages.co/enthrallinghistory/

Once you do, it will be intuitive. Enjoy, and thank you!

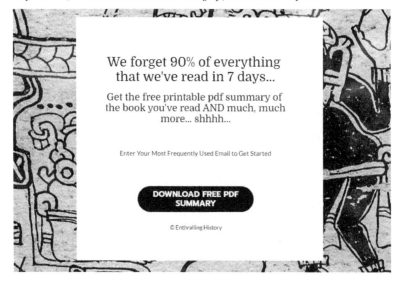

Appendix A: Further Reading and Reference

Harper, Rob. *Fighting the French Revolution: The Great Vendée Rising*. 2019.

Hibbert, Christopher. *The Days of the French Revolution*. 1980.

Klar, Jeremy. *The French Revolution, Napoleon, and the Republic*. 2015.

Salvemini, Gaetano. *The French Revolution: 1788-1792*. 1954.

Schama, Simon. *Citizens: A Chronicle of the French Revolution*. 1989.

Yonge, Charles. *The Life of Marie Antoinette*. 1876.

Printed in Great Britain
by Amazon

31254126R00050